Writing to the Prompt

A Guide to Answering Writing
Prompts Effectively

Candace P. Cooper

D1369756

Ruby Tree Publishing

Ruby Tree Publishing
7000 Independence Suite #160
BOX #127
Plano, TX 75025
www.rubytreepublishing.com

Printed in the United States of America

ISBN - 978–0–615–60055–0

Table of Contents

Special Thanks

It takes a village to raise English major. There have been several supportive professors and teachers along the way. They have not only served as instructors, but they have also been colleagues and friends. Special thanks, to Dr. Patricia Williams, my thesis director and mentor, who taught me to write while finding my voice as a scholar. Dr. Elizabeth Brown-Guillory, Dr. Lawrence Hogue, and Dr. Steven Pitts gave me many of the course based questions that helped me to consider this book.

Dr. Alan Ainsworth, Dr. Nellie Boyd, Dr. Rhonda Saldivar, Dr. Rufus Foster, Dr. Cathleen Tyson – Ferrol, Lana Reese, Betty Cox and Beverly Hixon invited me to explore my passion for composition while teaching at Texas Southern University and Houston Community College. They have been there to help me with teaching strategies and have given me invaluable feedback, and for that, I am eternally grateful.

I am truly indebted to the professors who have traveled with me during my teaching tenure and who have shared many ideas and thoughts during "formal" AND "cubicle" meetings. Dr. Charlene Evans, Krystal Berry, Amani Francis, Quiana Glapion, Brian Mack, Minnie Thomas, Brian Anderson, Ron Burnett, and Dr. Bennie Richards have co-labored with me in the field of English, Reading and Writing over the past decade, and our iron sharpening experiences have made me stronger.

My family has been a constant support throughout the process of penning this book. Their love motivates me, and their ideas quietly inspire me. They have been patient and selfless to allow me to write and reflect. To them, I dedicate this book.

Introduction

When I first entered college at the University of Houston, over 15 years ago, I was given a random test immediately following freshman orientation. Although it was similar to the test I'd taken to exit high school, I was overwhelmed with anxiety about taking a college entrance exam. I was not prepared.

When I thumbed through the test, (back then it wasn't computerized) thoughts of fear and uncertainty overshadowed my thinking. In fact, I clearly remember thinking that I should have paid more attention in Geometry and Algebra II. To my surprise, I also discovered that I was completely unprepared to answer the writing prompt before me. The prompt asked me if I thought that public school students in Texas should be required to wear school uniforms. It gave me the sociological background about the debate, and it told me to make my appeal to a state senator. It did not tell me how the essay should be structured or developed, nor did it tell me that the information used in the writing prompt could be used in my essay. I felt lost for a moment, but then as I had with every other writing test, I began to write.

I wrote mainly from my 18 year old rebellious teenage heart in opposition to the school uniform bill. I began the essay by writing without brainstorming, and I ended it just in time to leave the testing center to meet my friends to go to the mall. That's all I remember. That is all of the effort I gave. I thought that I performed well on the essay, because I was a good English student, but I did not know for sure. I waited for the results and was relieved when I passed the writing test. With math, on the other hand, even with the multiple choice options in front of me, I wasn't as lucky. I had to take Developmental Math, but that is another story for another day.

When I was admitted to the University of Houston, and began my freshman year was surprised to see how many written tests I had. I had to write exams not only in English, but also in History, Political Science, Psychology, and Theater. Although I was at the university on a journalism scholarship, I struggled to write for exams. Short essays and short answers challenged me because I wasn't sure what my professors wanted, and I did not understand how to respond. I had to read writing prompts and apply information I'd learned in class, and I also had to understand what the writing prompt desired. I found that I was answering prompts intuitively, from my feelings and passions, and not academically in the structure that professors preferred. I was able to manage my English Composition I class and made an "A". However, my secret ignorance regarding how to effectively answer writing prompts, from an academic perspective, was exposed in English Composition II when we had to explore writing from a rhetorical perspective.

At the age of 19, I understood that although I made A's in English Literature in high school, I was not taught to write. I had not learned how to answer questions posed to me in an academic context although I was trained to give my opinion passionately whether it was in three paragraphs or five paragraphs. In high school and middle school, sentence structure was not heavily scrutinized, and I only knew a few comma rules. I did not know that there were different types of lead-ins above and beyond the famous "eye catcher". I did not realize that crafting essays is a layered experience. It is like dressing appropriately based upon the weather and occasion. The thought process is similar choosing accessories to accent your attire. I realized that writing when fused with reading is the ultimate power because reading increases knowledge and writing supports or refutes it. I found that once I knew the format professors preferred in their written tests, I was powerful. I moved from a "C" student to an "A" student quickly.

In my junior year, I made the Dean's List for the first time because I figured out how to fuse my reading and writing together to answer my professors' test questions. This revolutionized my approach to test taking. I no longer thought that I was "cheating" by using information from the prompt in my essays. Instead, I realized that professors want specific things in their written responses. I started making "A's" in college and I never looked back.

This book is dedicated to students who want to perform well not only on tests, but also on daily assignments and quizzes. Many strategies I learned in college in addition to what I learned from the success of the students I have been privileged to teach over the last decade are in this book. I dedicate this book to them. Their graduation announcements, emails, and testimonies inspire me to continue to teach writing. It is their success that encouraged me to pen this book.

For those who have the desire to score well on written exams, I hope this book illuminates a path to academic success. I wish you well on your journey toward academic excellence. I believe that you will be empowered to write effectively to your audiences as you respond to an infinite number of questions posed in prompts.

Ruby Tree Publishing ©

Understanding Writing Prompts
Classroom Exams

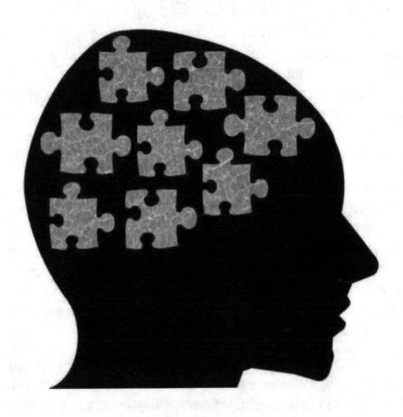

4

Chapter 1

Understanding Writing Prompts
Classroom Exams

Before we tackle writing prompts, we must first discover more about the purpose of the writing prompt.

What is prompt writing? Prompt writing means listening to or reading someone else's question or idea, thinking about it and responding. Prompt writing is important because it makes you think about what is important to another person and engage their topic with your ideas. It is basically how the world functions primarily because "a man is not an island unto himself." In order to be an active part of the world, you and I will have to think about questions that we do not pose and find solutions to problems that we did not create. Writing prompts are a part of life, and it is the way that educators test students' ability to read, reason and write.

Standardized tests, or departmental exams, can be overwhelming because often much of your success for the entire school year, or semester, will be judged solely on the grade you receive on the test.

Course Based Exams

In high school and college, written responses are regularly assigned in classes that are based in the humanities, fine arts and social sciences. Courses in English, History, Theater, Art, Psychology, and Political Science regularly require their students to explain or defend a theory. These theories are learned through reading, but they are challenged through the student's analysis of the subject matter.

Reading Assignments, Tests, and Quizzes

Oftentimes, the instructor tests the analysis of the theory, discussed in class, though a written response to a writing prompt. In some cases, it will include preliminary reading from a text book or maybe a even novel. These reading assignments are prime targets for writing prompts.

Instructors move beyond basic reading comprehension, which can be tested on multiple choice exams, to get to the heart of what the student actually learned in the assigned reading and homework. They want to know if the information was understood.

They also are interested in what conclusions, if any, were drawn from the reading assignment. More than that, they want to know if you, the student, are able to provide a logical explanation, whereby, defending the theory that was posed or refuting the theory altogether. Evaluating the true comprehension and analytical skills of the test taker with questions posed in a writing prompts accomplishes this goal.

In some instances, you may have an essay to complete outside of class on a given topic or theory. In other cases, you will have an in class exam on the subject matter. Whichever you are faced with, you need to know how to understand your assigned task and carry it out with confidence.

Final Exams, Midterms, and In Class Exams

Course based exams such as Midterm Exams and Final Exams, general tests and quizzes, pose three major challenges to test takers.

Ruby Tree Publishing ©

There are two different types of tests. There are tests that you study for, and there are tests that you don't. In many course based exams, students have the chance to study the information for the test. On other course based exams the student will receive a general writing prompt similar to what is given for standardized tests. This type of exam is usually given in composition classes because these classes focus squarely on writing essays. The approach for both tests is similar and present similar challenges.

Sample Writing Prompt from a Literature Class

Below is an example of a course based Midterm examination for a college literature class. This class has studied three sections in their textbook on African American Literature. The class does not know specifically what the test will cover, but they have studied literary texts from the 1700's to the 1930's which includes the Vernacular Period, the Pre-Post Civil War Literature, and the Harlem Renaissance.

English 2301
African-American Literature Final Examination
3 HOURS

Using our textbook, *The Norton Anthology of African American Literature*, please compose two short essays for ***both*** the following questions:

1. Compare and/or Contrast Spiritual and Gospel music in the Vernacular Tradition. Cite songs from each genre to support your thesis.

2. Discuss the major tenets of "The Atlanta Exposition Address" by Booker T. Washington and "Of Mr. Washington and Others" by W.E.B. Dubois. In your explanation, clearly state if you favor Washington or Dubois as it relates to the future of the Black race during the post Civil War period. Use the texts listed on our syllabus to explain your major points.

Assume that this is your course, and you have studied the material. Still, responding to this prompt presents a few obvious challenges.

THREE PROMPT CHALLENGES

Challenge #1 – Time

The test taker has only 3 hours to write 2 "short" essays which will require textual citations from a textbook.

Challenge #2 – Length

How long is a short essay exactly? What is acceptable for a sophomore level English Literature midterm examination?

Challenge #3 – Content

How should the comparison and contrast essay be structured?

What does "discuss" mean? Should the essay start with the discussion of the "major tenets" first and then persuade, or should the test taker persuade first and then discuss the major tenets? What does "vernacular" and "genre" mean?

Budgeting Time

When reading prompts, it is always appropriate to notice how much time you have. Typically, the amount of time allotted for an exam determines how much content you should write. The author of the literature test in the example above gives the class *3 hours* to compose *2 short essays*. Therefore, it is logical to deduce that each essay should take approximately 1½ hours to complete.

Ruby Tree Publishing ©

Essay Timeline Guidelines

1 HOUR EXAM - 1½ HOUR EXAM

5 – 10	minutes reviewing the prompt(s)
10-15	minutes brainstorming/outlining
45-60	minutes writing the draft
15-20	minutes revising and proofreading
0	minutes re-writing a final draft

Double space the first draft, then revise /edit it instead of writing a new draft. Writing a new draft wastes time.

Length Guidelines

Paragraph development and essay structure are essential components to composing excellent papers. The average content and structure lengths for college level compositions are as follows:

Length Guidelines

Paragraphs

Short answer paragraph	7-10 sentences
Well developed paragraph	10-20 sentences

Short Essays

3 well developed paragraphs which include an introduction, body and a conclusion

Standard Essays

5 well developed paragraphs which include an introduction, 3 body paragraphs, and a conclusion

9

Content Guidelines

Although standardized tests typically ask for a persuasive essay, college level tests require much more as is the case in the Literature test writing prompt. The test taker in this situation must write a comparison and contrast essay as well as an argument essay. Understanding the criteria is very important. *The first step is to understand the purpose for writing.* The purpose for writing not only decides your motive, but it also sets your tone and determines your vocabulary.

The Purpose for Writing

In some cases the purpose for writing is ***to inform,*** as is in the case of the comparison/contrast, cause/effect, process analysis, classification and definition essay.

In other cases it is ***to convince*** the reader to see the writer's point of view as is the case in persuasive essay and argument essay.

The purpose for writing could also be ***to entertain*** your reader by telling a story or describing an event as is the case in the narrative and descriptive essay.

Whatever the case, the reasons for writing and formulating your content in a specific way are determined by the writing prompt.

The Patterns of Organization

When students know the vocabulary of the writing prompt, they are more prepared to write appropriate answers to prompts. The prompt writer is asking the test-taker to respond to a given question in a particular format by using a certain pattern of development. The pattern of development is called a ***rhetorical mode.***

Ruby Tree Publishing ©

Rhetorical modes, as the word rhetoric suggests, make a case based upon a certain pattern of reasoning in an effort to persuade or impress. When writers answer a test question, they are reasoning with the grader who serves as their audience. The method they use to make their appeal varies in purpose.

The primary rhetorical modes, or patterns of organization are, argument, persuasive, comparison and contrast, cause and effect, narration, description, process analysis, illustration, process, division and classification and definition.

Each of the rhetorical modes has a specific purpose based upon the goals of the writing prompt. There is a certain pattern of organization that the author of the prompt wants. Your goal as a writer is to explain the information in the appropriate pattern. The test giver is testing your ability to reason within the pattern required.

Ruby Tree Publishing ©

Patterns of Organization

ARGUMENT	• to convince using logic and reason
PERSUASIVE	• to convince using biased perspectives
COMPARISON/CONTRAST	• to explain similarities and/or differences
CAUSE AND EFFECT	• to explain the reason something happens and the results
NARRATION	• to tell a story
DESCRIPTION	• to describe by using the five senses
PROCESS ANALYSIS	• to explain how to do something
ILLUSTRATION	• to explain a concept by using several examples
CLASSIFICATION/DIVISION	• to classify and categorize
DEFINITION	• to explain concept by defining it whereby using synonyms, antonyms and figurative language to expound on it

What does it mean when the writer says **evaluate?** It means to give the advantages and disadvantages with your opinion.

What does mean when the prompt says **discuss?** It means give reasons with pros and cons.

What does it mean when a prompt says **explain?** It means give the reasons or situations.

Understanding these key words can be the difference in passing and failing a test or a class. It is important that you know what the prompt requests and that you answer appropriately. The next chart provides information that helps decode action words used in many writing prompts.

Patterns of Organization
Key Words

Comment "Discuss breifly"	**Compare** Ephasize similarities but also present differences	**Contrast** Give differences only
Define Give meaning but no details	**Demonstrate** Show or prove and opinion, evaluation or judgement	**Describe** State the particulars in detail
Differentiate Show how things are different	**Discuss** Give reasons with "pros and cons" with details	**Evaluate** Discuss advantages and disadvantages with your opinion
Explain Give reasons, happenings or situations	**Give an example** Give a concrete example from a textbook or experience	**Identify** List and describe
Illustrate Give and example	**Interpret** State the meaning in simpler terms, using your judgement	**Justify** Prove or give reasons
Prove Give evidence and reasons	**Relate** Show how things interconnect	**Show** List your evidence in order of time, importance and logic
State List main points breifly without details	**Summarize** Organize and bring together the main points only	**Support** Back up a statement with facts and proof

Ruby Tree Publishing ©

Unfamiliar Words

Writing prompts will include language and concepts both familiar and unfamiliar to you. In most testing situations, you will have a *dictionary* and *thesaurus* available to you. It is a good idea to look up the unfamiliar word(s) to ensure you understand exactly what the writing prompt is asking. Using a thesaurus will allow you to not only find synonyms and antonyms of the unfamiliar word to help you establish meaning, but it will also give you words that you can use in your essay when you respond to the prompt. It is imperative that you take the time to look up unfamiliar words.

In cases where you do not have access to a dictionary or thesaurus or where the meaning of the word is different than what is offered in both reference books, then you should rely on *context clues*. Using the words that are surrounding the unfamiliar word will help to guide you to a general meaning of the unfamiliar word. It will also help you to grasp the true concept of what you should write.

Let's consider a question from our original example from the African American Literature Midterm Examination.

English 2301
African-American Literature
Final Examination
3 HOURS

Using our textbook, *The Norton Anthology of African American Literature*, please compose two short essays for *both* the following questions:
1. Compare and/or Contrast Spiritual and Gospel music in the Vernacular Tradition. Cite songs from each genre to support your thesis.

Ruby Tree Publishing ©

2. Discuss the major tenets of "The Atlanta Exposition Address" by Booker T. Washington and "Of Mr. Washington and Others" by W.E.B. Dubois. In your explanation, clearly state if you favor Washington or Dubois as it relates to the future of the Black race during the post Civil War period. Use the texts listed on our syllabus to explain your major points.

1. Compare and/or Contrast Spiritual and Gospel music in the **Vernacular** Tradition. Cite songs from each genre to support your thesis.

The question asks you to compare and contrast spiritual and gospel music in the vernacular tradition.

The word "vernacular" is an unfamiliar term. What words in the example question could help you figure out the meaning of "Vernacular"?

IDENTIFY THE CONTEXT CLUES IN THE SPACE BELOW

_____   _____

_____   _____

If you chose Spiritual, Gospel, music and Tradition, you were correct.

What do these words have in common? Spiritual and Gospel music are types of music. Both of these styles of music are meant to be sung and both have lyrics. Music and tradition are simply support words used to contextualize the question. Music is a part of the vernacular tradition.

What do you think Vernacular means?

_____

Ruby Tree Publishing ©

Vernacular:

Merriam Webster's Dictionary defines vernacular as:
Using a language or dialect native to a region or country rather than a literary, cultured, or foreign language.
Relating to, or being the normal spoken form if a language relating to, or characteristic of a period, place or group

In this case, the vernacular tradition is a timeframe in African American culture that speaks to God being the center of African American culture which is expressed through the Spirituals and Gospel Music affiliated with the period.

Also, you can look at the **root** of a word to help to determine an unknown word.

The Latin form of the word *vernaculus* includes the root *verna* means "slave born in the master's house." This information is helpful because it speaks to the period in question. The vernacular tradition in the questions specifically speaks to the Early African American Literature. The Spiritual Era is affiliated with slave culture (which is before 1875) and the Gospel Era is the time period immediately following the freeing of the slaves.

A student in the African American Literature class could logically, deduce this information if they (moderately) attended class for the first half of the academic semester and used context clues to answer the question.

There is another troublesome word in this prompt. The word "genre" is not a word that most people use every day. Therefore, it requires exploration. Let's look at the example prompt again.

17

1. Compare and/or Contrast Spiritual and Gospel music in the Vernacular Tradition. Cite songs from each **genre** to support your thesis.

This time, solve for the word genre.

What do you think "genre" means?

Definition of Genre

_____

_____

_____

Merriam Webster's Dictionary definition of genre is:
A particular type or category of literary, musical or artistic composition

From Webster's Thesaurus, you can gather additional clues:
Synonyms for genre include: kind, breed, class, description, sort, and type.

When you substitute the word "genre" with another word that has a similar meaning like "type", then the example prompt makes more sense. The test taker can deduce that the word genre refers to the "types of music".

1. Compare and/or Contrast Spiritual and Gospel music in the Vernacular Tradition. Cite songs from each genre to support your thesis.

With all of the new information in mind, can you figure out what the writing prompt question is asking now?

Ruby Tree Publishing ©

On the next few lines, paraphrase the writing prompt by putting it in your own words:

_____

_____

_____

Even though you may not know anything about the topic, do you think you could create a thesis statement using the information in the writing prompt?

What would you say?

_____

_____

_____

_____

_____

_____

Remember!

Understanding the writing prompt requires careful reading. Do not be afraid to look up unknown words in a dictionary or thesaurus. Looking up the unknown words or using context clues will not only help you understand what the writing prompt is asking, but it will also help you form a guiding statement for your answer to the prompt.

Chapter 2

Understanding Writing Prompts
Standardized Tests

Chapter 2

Understanding Writing Prompts
Standardized Tests

Standardized tests, and other forms of tests where you are not privy to any of the information that will be asked, follow a similar thought process as course based exams. Like the course based exam test questions from the African American Literature Class in the last chapter, you must read, understand, analyze, and prepare to write for a specified purpose.

Often, when students approach the writing section of these types of tests, they feel a certain amount of anxiety and trepidation because they are unfamiliar with the topic or because they are uninterested in the subject matter.

If you find yourself in this situation, you have to be creative in responding to the prompt.

Just as in course based testing, students will have to read the prompt for complete understanding. To illustrate the how this is done, let's look at a sample prompt from a standardized test.

Consider the following example:

READ AND ANALYZE THE FOLLOWING ESSAY PROMPT

Some people have said that the schools in the United States are not as good as the schools in other countries because students do not spend enough time in school. The United States Board of Education is trying to decide whether to have students go to school on Saturday mornings in order to give them more time to learn.

Ruby Tree Publishing ©

> *Write an essay a explaining why there should or should not be school on Saturday mornings for elementary, middle and high school students in the United States of America.*

Students who read this prompt may question if they can respond effectively. There are a few factors that make them hazardous.

THREE PROMPT CHALLENGES

Challenge #1 – Determining your level of interest
How can I write on this subject when I am not interested in it? What if I don't have an opinion?

Challenge #2 – Knowing both sides of the issue
Why would anyone want to agree to this or disagree with this?

Challenge#3 – Identifying subject, audience and purpose
What specifically is my topic? Who is my audience? Should I write to the people who are mentioned in the prompt, or should I really write to the person who is grading this essay? Why am I writing this? What is the purpose? Is it to inform or convince?

Determining your level of interest

The level of interest in a subject can distort your interpretation of the writing prompt. Test takers often scan the writing prompt before actually reading it. If they like the prompt, they passionately begin to write. When they are passionate, they usually write papers that have a lot of content. These papers are long but generally lack structure, and therefore, fail to adequately develop the topic in a logical way. They have to organize their information through outlining to ensure adequate development.

However, if a test taker discovers that they have a topic that is either not challenging or irrelevant to them, they try to get rid of the prompt by answering it quickly just to get it over with. Both responses gamble with prospect of receiving a passing grade.

Because the writing prompt solicits an emotional response from the reader, the test taker is bound to feel an emotion one way or the other. The problem arises for the test taker when they are unfamiliar with the subject matter, or they are indifferent toward the topic altogether. Brainstorming will help you, the test taker, to feel more comfortable and confident about the topic.

The solution to indifference is brainstorming

Brainstorming, which is also known as prewriting, is the key to adjusting your level of interest to a workable place. Asking journalist questions, (who, what, when, where, why and how) will aid in looking at the topic from several perspectives. This will help you understand the prompt and respond accordingly. We will discuss more about brainstorming in the next chapter.

Knowing both sides of the issue

True logic and reasoning is based in understanding. When you seek to achieve understanding, you should look at a concept from several angles. It is important to look at any persuasive, or argument based, writing prompt from both sides of the issue to get a true understanding of your position on the subject. Once you have considered all sides of the question posed in the prompt, you will be poised to write a strong argument. It will be very convincing because it is well thought out and logical. It only takes a few minutes during the brainstorming process to consider both sides.

Identifying the subject, audience and purpose

Considering the audience, purpose and occasion is a key factor in passing a written standardized test. The **audience**, or the person or people you are writing to, will determine if your subject matter is appropriate. On high school standardized tests and college entrance tests, students are often asked to write a letter to a school administrator, a board member, a civic leader, or a politician. In these instances, the audience is clearly stated.

On other non-course based standardized tests or on course based departmental exams, students are expected to take a position on a specific topic and explain it to an audience of educators. The specific audience is not identified. However, their instructions clearly indicate that the essay will be read by "two readers." The student should assume that the readers who will assign them holistic grade are people who are well educated and capable of determining if a student is ready for college or ready for the next level of English composition. Therefore, the audience, by default is a well educated English guru who has good credentials. The vocabulary and subject matter that the student chooses should be excellent. Slang, poor sentence structure and poor organization will merit failing grade on exams.

Professors and educators, who are often the authors of standardized tests and departmental exams, ask students to take a position on a subject, given through a well-crafted writing prompt, which asks for specific information. Therefore the purpose, or the reason for writing, is to persuade through explanation. Writing a good persuasive essay involves determining exactly what the writing prompt is asking and addressing the **occasion** for writing. The key to writing exactly what is asked is analyzing the prompt properly.

24

READ AND RESPOND TO
THE FOLLOWING DEPARTMENTAL FINAL EXAM
WRITING PROMPT
"TECHNOLOGY AND SOCIETY"

Do the benefits of technology outweigh the risks? Technological advances have lengthened human life, allowed people to travel in space, and enabled us to communicate with one another from any place on earth. But technology can also consume enormous amounts of natural resources, pollute the environment, or be used to create powerful weapons of war.

Your purpose is to write an essay, to be read by a classroom instructor, in which you analyze the impact of a particular technological advance on modern society.

In your response, select one of the following technological innovations: the telephone, the computer, the automobile, the television, the tractor, the skyscraper, or the nuclear power plant.

Discuss the advantages and/or disadvantages of that technology for individuals and society. Be sure to support your analysis with logical arguments and appropriate examples.

FILL IN THE FOLLOWING LINES BASED UPON THE DEPARTMENTAL FINAL EXAM WRITING PROMPT

INDENTIFY

SUBJECT_____

_____

AUDIENCE_____

_____

PURPOSE_____

_____

Ruby Tree Publishing ©

WHAT ARE THE KEY WORDS TO DETERMINE THE SUBJECT?_____

HOW DO YOU KNOW THE AUDIENCE? WHAT ARE YOUR CLUES?

_____

_____

IS THERE MORE THAN ONE PURPOSE FOR WRITING? WHAT WORDS SHOULD YOU PAY ATTENTION TO IN THE WRITING PROMPT TO HELP YOU DETERMINE YOUR *PURPOSE* FOR WRITING AND *PATTERN OF ORGANIZATION?*

_____

_____

_____

_____

EXTRA PRACTICE

FORMULATE A THESIS STATEMENT, WHICH IS THE MAIN IDEA OF THE ESSAY, AND 3 MAJOR REASONS THAT SUPPORT YOUR THESIS STATEMENT BASED UPON THIS WRITING PROMPT.

_____

_____

_____

_____

_____

_____

_____

_____

SAMPLE PROMPT FROM A COLLEGE PLACEMENT TEST
"ELECTIVE COURSES"

A School Board is concerned that the state's requirements for core courses in mathematics, English, science, and social studies may prevent students from taking important elective courses like music, other languages, and vocational education. The School Board would like to encourage more high school students to take elective courses and is considering two proposals. One proposal is to lengthen the school day to provide students with the opportunity to take elective courses. The other proposal is to offer elective courses in the summer.

Write a letter to the School Board in which you argue for lengthening the school day or for offering elective courses during the summer, explaining why you think your choice will encourage more students to take elective courses.

FILL IN THE FOLLOWING LINES BASED UPON THE COLLEGE PLACEMENT WRITING PROMPT

APPLY

WHAT ARE THE KEY WORDS TO DETERMINE THE SUBJECT?

_____

_____

WHO IS YOUR AUDIENCE? WHAT ARE YOUR CLUES?

_____

_____

_____

_____

_____

_____

27

IS THERE MORE THAN ONE PURPOSE FOR WRITING? WHAT ARE KEYWORDS IN THE WRITING PROMPT THAT HELP YOU DETERMINE YOUR PURPOSE FOR WRITING AND PATTERN OF ORGANIZATION?

_____

_____

_____

_____

EXTRA PRACTICE

FORMULATE A THESIS STATEMENT AND 3 MAJOR REASONS TO SUPPORT YOUR THESIS STATEMENT BASED UPON THIS WRITING PROMPT.

_____

_____

_____

_____

_____

_____

_____

_____

_____

_____

_____

_____

_____

_____

_____

_____

DID YOU CONSIDER YOUR SUBJECT, AUDIENCE AND PURPOSE? IF YOU MISSED SOMETHING, REVISE.

_____

_____

_____

_____

_____

_____

_____

_____

Based upon your response, check to make sure your subject and purpose relate to the prompt. Underline the keywords that relate to the prompt in the revised thesis statement above. List them in on the following lines.

_____

_____

_____

_____

_____

_____

_____

CHAPTER 3
Preparing to Write

Ruby Tree Publishing ©

CHAPTER 3
Preparing to Write

Most people think that you should just dive into a written test immediately after scanning a prompt. Writing without thinking through your topic in a methodical way may save you time, but it is not beneficial in the long run. Many students feel paralyzed and do not know what to say or how to say it, so they write almost nothing. Or they write something so vague or general to where it does not show depth or critical thinking. Many students feel as if they have writers block, and their mind draws a blank. Others feel as if they are ill and cannot focus. If you have had any of these symptoms, you have suffered from test anxiety or writer's block.

Overcoming Test Anxiety and Writer's Block

Many students suffer from test anxiety. Some people are diagnosed, and they know they suffer with it, while others just feel sick and suffer with nausea, shaky hands, sweating, dry mouth or in some cases a rapid heartbeat. Psychologists believe that this condition is caused by other conditions like depression, low self esteem, racing thoughts while testing, and negative talk about one's abilities. Any of these factors may contribute greatly to test anxiety and cause poor grades on written tests.

Students who have these challenges can offset their chances of success by focusing on how bad they feel about themselves and how badly they want to avoid the test.

Solutions to Test Anxiety and Writer's Block are found in brainstorming. Free writing will help test takers who suffer from test anxiety feel more comfortable if they use at least 10 minutes of their testing time to process their emotions and fears on paper.

Ruby Tree Publishing ©

While writing about their fears on a separate paper (away from their test), they can honestly process their feelings of fear before they address the test question. This can be a part of their brainstorming activity and should only take about 10-15 minutes – which is the amount of time suggested for brainstorming activities. This is a great way to overcome writer's block and test anxiety while dual processing the writing prompt.

If you have test anxiety and are not able to have extra "scratch paper" during the test or if there is not enough time during the testing situation to process your feelings of fear, then you will have to carve out time BEFORE you enter the testing center to process your feelings. Whichever situation you are faced with, you will need time to write about your feelings so that you can focus on the task at hand.

Overcoming writer's block in the absence of test anxiety is cured through brainstorming in a methodical way. Brainstorming is the first step of the writing process for a good reason. It helps to get your ideas flowing as it also helps you to focus on a topic and explore it from a variety of angles.

There are several ways to brainstorm – and all of them are good. However, there is one technique that really allows you to think 360° around a topic so that you can arrive at the best explanation of your subject matter. Since you only need to spend approximately 10-15 minutes brainstorming, you will need a technique that will use your time effectively.

Journalist Questions

Questioning is the best way to arrive at answers quickly. Relying on the basic, WHO, WHAT, WHEN, WHERE WHY and HOW will allow you to think about your subject matter from several angles. Paired with other traditional forms of brainstorming, such as *mapping, clustering, and listing,* questioning is an excellent way to explore your thoughts. Critical thinking, questioning your ideas, and moving beyond yourself is important when addressing a prompt. Remember, you need ideas, and you need them quickly. You only know a limited amount of information on a given topic, so *questioning allows you to think 360° around a subject.*

For example, consider the following writing prompt:

"Same Sex Adoptions"

Write a paragraph addressing whether or not the legal system in the United States should force adoption agencies to allow qualified same-sex couples to adopt children of the same gender. You may use illustrations and observations to support your views.

33

First, ask yourself questions about the concept of "Same Sex Adoption".

WHO

When you think about adoption, you think about people. Therefore, the question "who" immediately comes to mind. You may ask yourself, "Who would be involved in this adoption process?" You may also ask, "Who would be affected by the adoption?" These types of questions are simple questions which seem meaningless. However, they are important to exploring the topic because they make you think about the people involved in the writing prompt, not just your personal perspective.

WHAT

Next, you would ask, "what"? A natural question could be, "What is at stake?" What do I know about same sex couples? The answers to these questions may surprise you. We often think that we know how we feel about a topic based upon our initial emotional response. Just by asking "What do I know about same sex couples, you are forced to question your perspective. These types of inquiries force you to question why your belief system and values are what they are. It is important to tap in to your feelings about a prompt and think critically, because when you are honest about how you feel about a prompt, you are able to write more freely and efficiently. You will not run out of ideas when you are questioning what you believe and why you believe it.

Other questions like "when" and "where" create ideas like, "When will the adoption take place?" It asks, "Where would this type of family unit be acceptable, or where would it be unacceptable?" The answers to these questions will help you understand two points of view.

WHERE

In the case of the "Same Sex Adoption" writing prompt, the test taker would reconcile that different parts of the United States would view same sex marriage differently. For instance, perceived liberal states like California, New York, New Jersey and Pennsylvania, may be more welcoming of the idea of same sex marriage and same gender adoptions. However, more conservative states on the "Bible Belt" like Texas, Oklahoma, Mississippi, and Arkansas, may not agree to recognize same sex relationships as a way of life and would probably reject the idea.

WHEN

"When" makes you *question past, present and future*. Therefore, you are forced to move beyond what you see in your generation and look either to generations past and forward to generations in the future. This helps you to expand your point of view and move out of your comfort zone of "self" as you think and inquire about the lives of others in the past or future. This will give you new ideas and new ways to approach your topic as you visualize the past and future.

WHY

"Why" is the cornerstone of rhetoric! It is what the great philosophers asked themselves over and over and over again. In Webster's Dictionary, it is defined as "for what reason, cause or purpose?" Therefore, we need this question more than any when brainstorming. In regards to the "Same Sex Adoption" prompt, we may ask questions like, "Why is this important", Why would someone want this, or Why would the reject this?" This inquiry makes you question your motives and the motives of others. Proponents of same sex adoption may want it so that they can expand their family if they are in a homosexual relationship.

35

Opponents of the measure may feel that homosexuality is wrong and the effects of the relationship would be bad for the adopted child. Again, it forces you to look at the prompt's dilemma from a 360° perspective. You must look at the different angles to get true meaning.

HOW

When exploring "how" something is done, it requires a more practical approach than the philosophic approach suggested in the question "why". "How" simply asks the effects of something whereas "why" mostly deals with causes. In exploring "Same Sex Adoptions", we are forced to look at the impact of the adoption on the child, on the parents and on the nation as whole. Mostly, it begs the question of "how will the adoption affect the child" or "how will the adoption affect the country?" The lifestyle would suggest changing what is considered the norm in American culture where mostly heterosexual couples raise children of both genders. Reconstructing this idea would certainly be cause for consideration from someone writing this essay. Nevertheless, one would also find that the adoption level would increase and more children would have parents. Both of these considerations are appropriate when addressing this prompt. Again, you are able to look at both sides of the issue before making a decision.

THINK 360° - Critical Thinking

Questioning allows you to think about your subject matter from different angles. It allows you to think critically and objectively so that you can write you best paper. When thinking of ideas, all ideas are good. Write them all down, regardless of how you feel about them. You may be able to use them later.

Instinctively, you will respond to the questions that are assigned to you in writing prompts. You will want to resist the idea of brainstorming and really thinking about what you are going to write.

You probably will not want to critique your ideas or do the additional work of thinking of the opposite perspective because you feel a strong conviction about your perspective. Regardless of how you feel, critically thinking about your topic. It will allow you to write a stronger paper because you can use the argument of the opposing side to your advantage. All you have to do is address their argument and then explain why you think your idea is better. It is a valuable skill that will extend beyond your essay writing years! **Remember to always THINK 360 °.**

JUST FOR FUN!

Are you a visual, kinesthetic or auditory learner?

Visual learners may be interested in the following types of jobs: architects, engineers, surgeons, artist, and designers.

Kinesthetic learners may be interested in the following types of jobs: surgeons, physical therapist, carpenter, mechanic, athlete, dancer, and actor.

Auditory Learners may be interested in the following types of jobs: counselors, ministers, politicians, teachers, marketing consultants, and salesperson.

Discover your learning style.
Visit
www.Learning-Styles-Online.com

Brainstorming Activities

Mapping and Clustering

CREATE A MAP WHERE YOU CAN EXPLORE YOUR SUBJECT

Adding circles to this map will help you to expand your ideas. You may ask specific questions or you may add or subtract circles to suit your needs. Creating branches may be helpful for those who are *visual or kinesthetic learners*. People who learn by looking at diagrams and pictures enjoy this process because it organizes the words into a picture as it aggregates the information. Kinesthetic learners appreciate this form of brainstorming because they are able to create new ideas and shapes at the same time.

Use the diagram above to practice mapping on the writing prompt about **"Same Sex Adoption"**. Create additional branches and circles to explore your thoughts on the controversial subject.

Ruby Tree Publishing ©

QUESTION BASED MAPPING AND CLUSTERING

Notice that the information in the topic area is a "watered down" basic form of the "Same Sex Adoption" writing prompt. The questions posed are not answered. They are simply stated. When completing a mapping and clustering diagram, you can put the complete question in the box (or a watered down version of it). Then, you can brainstorm and write your questions. This technique beats looking at your hands for 10 minutes trying to figure out what to write! Instead, kinesthetic learners can use their hands to create a well thought out response by using mapping through questioning.

Answering the questions posed on the mapping model is a quick exercise once the questions have been placed. Consider the following example bubble.

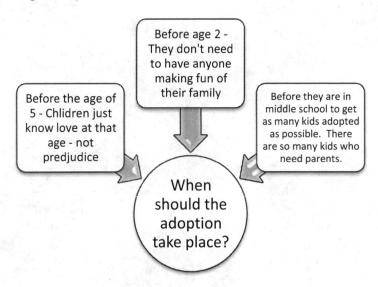

Before age 2 - They don't need to have anyone making fun of their family

Before the age of 5 - Chlidren just know love at that age - not predjudice

Before they are in middle school to get as many kids adopted as possible. There are so many kids who need parents.

When should the adoption take place?

Thinking critically is important. Notice how the writer suggests that the adoption should take place from age 2, to 5, to middle school. They had different perspectives and considered each of them. Now the test taker has plenty to write. They thought **360°**. Now it's your turn. Consider how you would respond to who, what, where, why, how?

Practice Mapping and Clustering

THINK 360°

Use the following diagrams to practice questioning on "Same Sex Adoption" writing prompt. Remember, you can add or more bubbles to your chart if necessary.

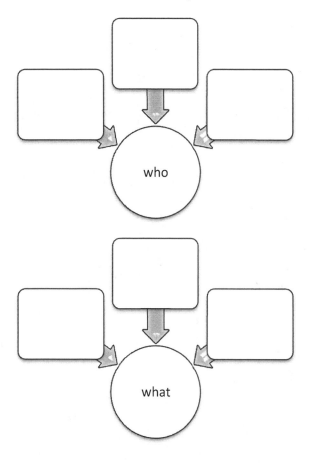

Ruby Tree Publishing ©

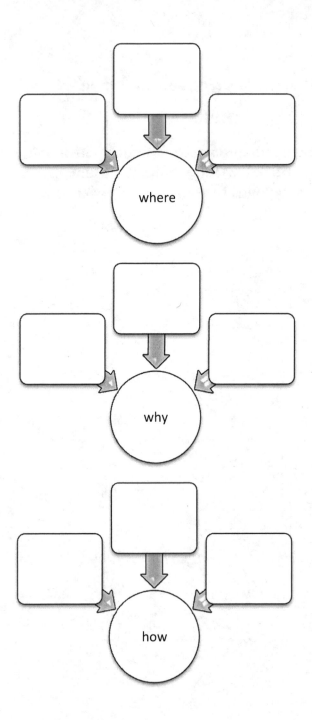

For those who enjoy making list to organize their ideas more quickly, then a column based brainstorming approach is ideal. With listing, you can use your topic as your header and complete columns below it. You can do it vertically as shown below or horizontally.

VERITICAL LISTING

Topic					
WHO	WHAT	WHEN	WHERE	WHY	HOW

Vertical listing is great for people who enjoy categorizing information and making lists. This method may appeal to visual learners because it feeds their need to organize information into small sections. Like mapping and clustering, it appeals to them because it allows them the necessary boundaries they need to see information. Unlike mapping and clustering, it allows them to section information without feeling confined. When reviewing the columns and questions in a chart format, the visual learner can not only create information more effectively, but also review the answers to their questioning process more efficiently so that they are able to write their outline or rough draft faster. See the chart below to see how questioning in vertical listing works.

Should adoption agencies in the United States be forced to allow same sex couples to adopt children of the same gender?					
Who is involved in the decision? Who will be effected most by the outcome?	What is at stake? What do I know about same sex couples?	When will the adoption take place. When will it effect the child most?	Where would this be acceptable? Where would this not be acceptable?	Why would someone want this? Why would someone reject it?	How would this impact the child in the long term. How would this impact the U.S?

For the visual learner, vertical listing is an excellent way to approach questioning. Notice that the answers to the questions are provided in a format that is easy to see and understand.

44

Practice Vertical Listing

THINK 360°

Complete the following chart using question. Use the "Same Sex Adoption" writing prompt to explore your ideas. If necessary, use additional paper.

Should adoption agencies in the United States be forced to allow same sex couples to adopt children of the same gender?					
INVOLVED -- Parents -- Courts EFFECTED MOST Adopted Children					

Ruby Tree Publishing ©

HORIZONTAL LISTING

Although auditory learners may opt for free writing as preferred method of brainstorming, they may enjoy the simplicity of brainstorming via horizontal listing. Horizontal listing allows the writer to make simple lists, but they are not confined by a "chart" or a "bubble". Instead, they are able to continuously explore their thoughts within a certain measure of structure.

Topic

- WHO
- WHAT
- WHEN
- WHERE
- WHY
- HOW

Because auditory learners can remember a great deal of what they hear, they tend enjoy listening to their thoughts and jotting them down. Questioning through horizontal listing is appealing because it gives them leeway to hear their thoughts clearly and structure them quickly.

Ruby Tree Publishing ©

Should adoption agencies in the United States be forced to allow same sex couples to adopt children of the same gender?

- Who is involved in the decision?
  Who will be effected most by the outcome?
- What is at stake?
  What do I know about same sex couples?
- When will the adoption take place.
  When will it effect the child most?
- Where would this be acceptable? Where would this not be acceptable?
- Why would someone want this?
  Why would someone reject it?
- How do I feel about this?
  How would this impact the child in the long term.
  How would this impact the U.S?

Notice that the questions are posed in a "free-form" format, and there is space to add more information without disrupting the flow of organization. This is appealing to learners *who hear the thoughts in their mind and write them down.*

Auditory learners typically have a lot to say and need help organizing their thoughts in a way that is meaningful. Once their thoughts are organized, they can easily write their rough draft. Oftentimes, auditory learners spend a lot of time revising their work because it is disorganized. They have said a lot, but it is not written clearly. They need help structuring. Horizontal Listing coupled with questioning will help them through the writing process more quickly and effectively. Now, it's you turn!

47

Practice Horizontal Listing

THINK 360°

Use the "Same Sex Adoption" writing prompt to answer the questions below. Feel free to ask and answer more questions in addition to the ones included in the exercise. You may use additional paper.

> Should adoption agencies in the United States be forced to allow same sex couples to adopt children of the same gender?

- Who will be effected most by the outcome?

- What do I know about same sex couples?

- When will it effect the child most?

- Where would this be acceptable? Where would this not be acceptable?

- Why would someone want this? Why would someone reject it?

- How do I feel about this?

48

Free writing and Questioning

Free writing is one of the most effective ways to explore a topic through questioning. Free writing does not require you to have essay or sentence structure, good spelling, or punctuation usage. It does not require you to remain focused on the subject matter. It simply requires writing. It is a method used in journaling and other forms of reflective writing. Using this method, not only can you ask questions, but you have the ability to answer them immediately. Moreover, you are not required to continue a line of questioning if you find that it is troublesome. Instead, you can quickly move to the next line of questioning. If you get nervous or anxious about the prompt, and are running out of things to say or questions to ask, the best part about free writing is that you can process your emotions as you question. This helps you to remain focused on the writing prompt while processing your anxiety.

Sample Student Free Writing Activity

Sometimes, students are given prompts they do not feel they can answer. It could be because they are not exposed to the information and have a limited perspective or they may not know enough about the subject matter to give them enough to discuss. This was the case with Michael, the student who wrote the following free writing brainstorming activity.

"New Levels of Success"

Many theologians have said that with each success, one experiences a new "devil". Christian evangelist Joyce Meyer, in her book "Battlefield of the Mind" coined the phrase, "New Level, New Devil" to discuss the chess game that occurs when people have to make adjustments to life's challenges. United States Secretary of State, Henry Kissinger, in 1979, said, "Each success only buys an admission ticket to a more difficult problem." Using your personal experience or the experience of someone you know, explain if you agree or disagree with this statement.

Ruby Tree Publishing ©

Sample Brainstorming Activity

Who do I know that's successful? My grandfather was successful. He didn't go the college, but he did serve in World War II. He always talked about how hard it was to serve in the war. He made it back home from Germany. He had tons of war stories. They always come out at the wrong time. Like when he was giving a sermon or at my brothers party. He made it back from the war, so I guess that is considered successful. What is considered success? Would he coming home from war be considered successful? Not getting hurt or killed in a war takes skill and God. When he got home he had a lot of kids to feed. He didn't have a job right away, but he got a job with the post office. During that time, my grandparents did not have much money to feed their kids. I guess that would be a new devil because he survived the war but was helpless to feed his family once he got home.

What am I supposed to be writing about again? I haven't really written much although I have a lot of words on the paper. Oh yeah, let me ask another question. How can success present a new problem? That seems like a dumb question. I had better hurry up and find an answer because I have to get started with my paper. Kissinger said that "each success only buys an admission ticket to a more difficult problem." What does this mean to me? I have bought admission tickets to carnivals and football games, but not necessarily to success. I wonder what made him say it like that. It reminds me of the time when I went to the amusement park with Natalie Jones. She was so pretty and it took me forever to ask her out. I finally did and she said yes. I took her on a date to the carnival. It took me two weeks to save up enough money to afford it, but I finally did. When we got to the carnival, I was so proud because no one else I was friends with could get her to go out with them. I remember that she wanted to go on every ride and eat all kinds of sweets. Who knew a girl like that could eat so much. I ended up spending all of my money, but my friends thought I was the man. She had so much fun, spending all of my money to where she asked me if we could go out the next week. I found that although I had the girl of my dreams, I had work more hours to keep her happy.

Because I worked more hours, I got a promotion at my job. I had to budget my time more at school so that I could study. Studying made me ready for college so I could keep a girl like Natalie around longer. I couldn't keep up with her, but I definitely see what Kissinger meant. Each time I got a promotion I got more responsibility and more notoriety. I think I'm ready to write.

PRACTICE:

Now, it is your turn. Practice one of the brainstorming techniques in this chapter to explore. Use the same prompt from the sample free writing brainstorming technique. Use the lines below to complete your brainstorming activity.

Example Writing Prompt

Many theologians have said that with each success, one experiences a new "devil". Christian evangelist Joyce Meyer, in her book "Battlefield of the Mind" coined the phrase, "New Level, New Devil" to discuss the chess game that occurs when people have to make adjustments to life's challenges. United States Secretary of State, Henry Kissinger, in 1979, said, "Each success only buys an admission ticket to a more difficult problem." Using your personal experience or the experience of someone you know, explain if you agree or disagree with this statement.

PRACTICE BRAINSTORMING

_____
_____
_____
_____
_____
_____
_____
_____
_____
_____
_____
_____
_____
_____
_____
_____
_____
_____
_____
_____
_____
_____
_____
_____
_____
_____
_____
_____
_____

Free writing should not be used as a final draft!

Free writing looks like an essay when it is completed, but it is NOT. It needs to be read, analyzed, synthesized, organized, and edited.

How to Use Free Writing to Complete Your Final Essay

Read - what you have written. Don't try to just edit the free writing and turn it in without reviewing it.

Analyze – see what you can use and what you need to discard.

Synthesize – make all of your ideas work together under a main idea of your essay.

Organize – put your ideas into an outline to make sure that your ideas or developed properly. Then write your essay. Revise it to make sure it is clear, focused, and logical

Edit - Look for capitalization, punctuation, spelling, and usage.

Free writing is a useful tool to writers who need to explore their thoughts about the prompt and their anxiety. It should not, however, be used in lieu of a well organized essay. Outlining is one of the best ways to prepare to write a well planned essay.

Outlining

After brainstorming via mapping, listing and free writing, organize your thoughts into a usable outline. The outline can be as simple or elaborate as you choose. Regardless of the detail involved, it should clearly give you blueprint of your paragraph or essay. A simple paragraph outline has four primary sections: an introductory statement, a topic sentence, examples and a conclusion statement.

54

Paragraph Outline

A. *Introductory Statement* (Attention Grabber)

B. *Topic Sentence* (Main idea of the paragraph)

C. *Example* (Support used to explain the topic sentence)

D. *Example* (Support used to explain the topic sentence)

E. *Example* (Support used to explain the topic sentence)

F. *Conclusion Statement* (Summarizes the main point of the paragraph)

Essay Outlines

Essay outlines are more intricate because they usually cover three to five paragraphs in testing situations. For research papers and other writing assignments, students may have to write several paragraphs over 5 - 15 pages. Like the standard five paragraph essay, the short essay has an introduction, a body paragraph and a conclusion.

Different tests will call for different types of essays. Short essay prompts will usually indicate that it should be a "short essay". It may use the phrases "short response" or "short explanation" while still requesting an essay. When these words are used, the test grader is looking for at least 3 examples and approximately 150-250 words. The standard essay structure is five paragraphs. Like the short essay, there is an introduction, body and conclusion. However, the information in the standard essay is more detailed. The body gives at least 9 examples and it is between 350-600 words long. The following essay outline structures can be used to organize your brainstorming activities into essay structure. These outlines can be modified to fit your personal writing style, but each paragraph must have a main idea and adequate examples.

Short Essay Outline

Introduction

A. Introductory Statement (Attention Grabber)

B. Thesis Statement (Main idea of the essay)

F. Conclusion Statement (Transition - leads into body paragraph)

Body

    A. Point 1

        1. Example

        2. Example

    B. Point 2

        1. Example

        2. Example

    C. Point 3

        1. Example

        2. Example

Conclusion

    A. Thesis Statement (Reflection)

    B. Point 1 (Reflection)

    C. Point 2 (Reflection)

    D. Point 3 (Reflection)

    E. Conclusion Statement (Reflect)

Essay Structure

A. Lead In

B Thesis Statement

C. Topic Sentence 1

D. Topic Sentence 2

E. Topic Sentence 3

F. Conclusion Statement

A. Topic Sentence 1

B. Example

C. Example

D. Example

E. Conclusion Statement

A. Topic Sentence 2

B. Example

C. Example

D. Example

E. Conclusion Statement

A. Topic Sentence 3

B. Example

C. Example

D. Example

E. Conclusion Statement

A. Thesis Statement (Reflect and Project)

B. Topic Sentence 1 (Reflect and Project)

C. Topic Sentence 2 (Reflect and Project)

D. Topic Sentence 3 (Reflect and Project)

E. Conclusion Statement (Reflect and Project)

Ruby Tree Publishing ©

Remember!

Outlining an important step in the brainstorming process because it allows the test taker to visualize their essay before they write it. It also provides a blue print for their work which will save time when selecting, adding and removing ideas while writing. Further, it saves time with revision. Revision, in the writing process, is intended to fix issues with essay content and logical flow. In outlining, the content is determined early, so logic is determined early. Choosing the ideas from brainstorming early will keep you focused and your ideas unified under the thesis statement. Outlining helps you to achieve logic and coherence early, so you can spend time proofreading time editing for punctuation, capitalization, spelling, subject/verb agreement, and other grammar errors. Because time is important when testing, it is important that every minute is carefully. Therefore, it is important to maximize your effort by brainstorming and organizing effectively. When this process is completed, it is time to write the first draft of your essay.

CHAPTER 4

WRITING AND REVISION

The second step in the writing process, after you have finished brainstorming and outlining, is writing the rough draft of your essay. It should take approximately 45 minutes to construct your draft if you are writing a standard essay.

A standard essay includes five paragraphs consisting of an introduction paragraph, three body paragraphs, and a conclusion paragraph. The **introduction** invites the reader into the essay with an introductory statement, also known as an "attention grabber" or "shocking statement". The lead in is a creative way hook your reader into your paper, and it is a smart way to introduce your **thesis**. The thesis is the central point of the essay. It is the guiding statement that clearly states your position regarding the charge given in the essay prompt.

The **body** of the essay includes three paragraphs which explain the thesis statement. Each **body paragraph**, or topic paragraph, includes a **topic sentence** which is considered the main idea of the body paragraph as well as **examples** that explain the topic sentence. The function of the body paragraph is to give detailed insight into the thesis statement. It should discuss the writing prompt directly and not stray off subject.

The **conclusion** of the essay is the cincher. It can summarize the major points of the essay or it can give readers more to consider regarding the subject matter in the future through a method called "reflect and project". Many times students do not close their essays effectively. It is important to close the essay with care, as it is the last thing the grader will read.

The Characteristics of the Rough Draft

Writing the rough draft of the essay is the second step in the writing process. It allows the writer to put the ideas derived in the brainstorming process into paragraph and essay structure in a more formal way. It does not have to be perfect, but because of time constraints imposed on many testing situations, *you will want to give as much time as possible to creating a near perfect draft early in the writing process.* Thinking through your thesis statement and topic sentences during the brainstorming process, by creating an outline, will help you with time management while writing and revising your essay.

Characteristics of Revision

Revision includes proofreading your work for content errors. In other words, you are looking for what is wrong with your paper based upon what you wrote and the way you developed your ideas. It is not **editing**, which is proofreading for capitalization, punctuation, spelling, grammar and usage. Revision searches for unity of ideas, adequate development of the topic, coherence of thought though organization, and effective communication.

Revising an essay involves searching for the following:

Unity – Make sure all of your ideas work together under the thesis statement or topic sentence.
Focus – stay focused on your topic and thesis statement
Clarity – Clearly explain your thoughts and ideas
Coherence – Explain your thoughts logically; arrange your ideas in the best logical order so that your points are effective.
Development – Develop your ideas by using at least 3 examples per paragraph and at least 3 paragraphs in a standard essay.

AVOID THESE PITFALLS AT ALL COST

ANNOUNCEMENTS

Writing an announcement such as, "This paragraph will explain" or "This paragraph will be about" is a major red flag and should be avoided at all costs. Instead, write a clear topic sentence that eliminates these unnecessary words and focuses on the subject proposed in the prompt and purpose for writing.

For example, instead of writing "This paragraph is about why people should vote for mandatory summer school," write "Mandatory summer school will help the United States become a stronger country because students will be more educated and more disciplined."

SHIFTING EMPHASIS OF IDEAS

Straying from the main idea will almost always assure a failing grade on an essay. Therefore, when revising, check each sentence to make sure it belongs in your paragraph. If it doesn't, take it out.

WORDINESS

Take out all unnecessary words. Wordy sentences may make your paragraphs seem longer, but they confuse the meaning of your sentences and often make for excessive grammatical errors.

UNCLEAR PRONOUN REFERENCES

Never start a sentence with the words "this" or "that". Your reader may not know what you mean. Starting sentences with "this" or "that" also is cause for writing a sentence fragment in certain cases.

CHAPTER 5

TOPIC SENTENCES
AND
THESIS STATEMENTS

Many times, especially on short answer exams where multiple questions are asked and where short, yet in depth, responses are expected, a concise well written **paragraph**, which is a group of related sentences intended to communicate on clear idea, is appropriate. However, when you must write on a larger scale develop a concept thoroughly, and prove a point of view in great detail, a well crafted **essay** is appropriate.

Topics, Topic Sentences, and Thesis Statements

Writing prompts have topics built in. They are typically found in the charge. For instance, consider the prompt:

> Do you think the SAT or ACT exam is an accurate measure of a student's aptitude for college? Support your position with specific examples.

The topic is already selected for you. You must write on the subject - *SAT and ACT exams as an accurate measure of a student's aptitude for college*. You will have to add your opinion to the subject to create a topic sentence. You will need to prove if they should or should not continue using the test as the measure of aptitude and support this position with several examples to prove your point. To do this, you would need to create a main idea for your paper whether it is for a short paragraph, or if it is for a longer essay.

Ruby Tree Publishing ©

The paragraph will contain the **topic**, which is the subject matter of the entire paper. Like the **thesis statement**, includes the subject assigned by the writing prompt, a **controlling idea**, which is your attitude or perspective about the writing prompt. When combined, the topic and controlling idea form the **topic sentence**, which is the main idea of the paragraph. The thesis statement differs from the topic sentence in that it is the main idea of an essay, and it is broad enough to cover a larger body of information. The topic sentence should be more specific, than a thesis statement because it covers a smaller body of information. The **examples**, or supporting details, are used to give more detailed information about your topic sentence. They provide the test-taker with the opportunity to develop their perspective about the topic. Although is it optional, it is good to close your paragraph with a **conclusion statement** as it brings finality to the information contained the body paragraph.

Topic Sentence vs. Thesis Statement

The topic sentence is *similar to* the thesis statement because both of them serve as the guiding statement.

The ***topic sentence*** is the main idea or guiding statement for the ***topic paragraph***.

The ***thesis statement*** is the main idea, or central point of an ***essay***.

The Role of the Topic Sentence

The topic sentence serves as the backbone of the paragraph, as it also serves as the primary tool of explanation for the thesis statement when it is a part of an essay.

Ruby Tree Publishing ©

The topic sentence, like the thesis statement, has two parts: *The topic*, which is provided in the writing prompt, and the *controlling idea*, which is the author's narrowed perspective of the topic. Creating a topic sentence for a paragraph is a simple formula if you pay attention to the details provided for you in the prompt.

The test maker knows exactly what they want. They want to hear "your take" on their subject matter.

The *topic* belongs to the *test maker*, but the *controlling idea* belongs to the *test taker*.

This relationship creates the balance required to produce a strong paper. The mission is to pass the test and receive a high grade, so you have to work within the parameters of the prompt.

Consider the following writing prompt:

**Sample Prompt
"In Service"**

In many countries, **citizens are required to serve in the military for a year or more. Do you believe the United States** should institute a **similar practice**? Why or why not? Use specific reasons and examples to support your answer.

The topic is embedded in the prompt. All of the clues for you to create a clear and focused topic sentence are hidden in the **lead in,** which is the *hook* or background information about the text. It is also found in the **charge**, which is the question the prompt asks you to consider. Both of these clues help to formulate your topic sentence because it squarely addresses the mission of the prompt.

Ruby Tree Publishing ©

The keywords in the *lead in* and *charge* can combine to create a topic sentence.

This **direct reference topic sentence** has clear topic that speaks directly to the prompt. With a topic sentence like this, you force yourself to write directly to the prompt, and you remain on subject.

An **indirect reference topic sentence** can also give you an effective topic sentence by using synonyms, paraphrasing and summarizing. This type of sentence is appropriate for college level writing and is preferred in humanities courses like English and History. This type of topic sentence requires skill and finesse.

If mishandled, it could cause the writer to veer off subject and head in a direction other than what is specifically requested in the writing prompt. Test takers must think carefully about their topic sentence, and thesis statements before using it as the guiding statement for their paper.

Synonyms, paraphrasing and summarizing are tools that can help the writer avoid "parroting" the prompt, but still give the information just the way the test maker intended it. With each of these replacement tools, the writer is able to refer to the prompt without repeating the exact language in the prompt.

Because synonyms are different words with the same or similar meanings, and paraphrasing takes someone's sentences and replaces them with new words that have the same meaning, test takers are able to re-create the premise of the prompt without using the exact words from the prompt. Summarizing, which is a common practice in writing, affords the test taker the opportunity to cut down on words and make the ideas shorter and easier to understand. Creating an indirect reference topic sentence requires an extra step in the creation process, but it is worth it.

Consider the following topic sentence based upon the sample prompt.

Sample Prompt
"In Service"

In many countries, citizens are required to serve in the military for a year or more. Do you believe the United States should institute a similar practice? Why or why not? Use specific reasons and examples to support your answer.

Americans operate from a place of entitlement when it comes to their country because they take their liberty and freedom for granted; it is time for United States citizens to become responsible and serve their country.

In the indirect reference topic sentence, the writing prompt's language is summarized and words are substituted. This is highly appropriate and recommended for college courses and standardized tests like the ACT and SAT. This is not necessarily required for middle school, high school or fundamental English courses at the college level. In these classes, foundational skills are required and students are expected to learn direct reference topic sentences first before elevating to indirect reference topic sentences.

The Controlling Idea

The controlling idea of this topic sentence is in italics. The controlling idea is the information that is not given in the prompt. Instead, it is the way the test taker feels about the charge posed in the prompt. It is a personal point of view. It narrows the topic so that the test taker can write what is important to him on the subject matter.

The Controlling Idea is Important for Two Reasons.

1. The controlling idea *narrows the topic* so that it is manageable.

2. The controlling idea makes the prompt interesting to the test taker because the *prompt specifically speaks to their point of view* when addressed through the controlling idea.

The United States *has a history of patriotism that has made its* **citizens** *the beneficiaries of freedom within its borders and abroad;* therefore, *it should be a* **requirement** *for all* **citizens** to **serve in the military for at least one year.**
The italicized controlling idea clearly shows that the test taker believes that patriotism and freedom, is important and that United States citizens should serve their country. The author's attitude about the question posed in the prompt is clear.

THINK 360°

PRACTICE: On a separate sheet of paper, brainstorm (using mapping, listing or free writing). Afterwards, below each of the writing prompts, create a *direct reference* topic sentence. Highlight your topic and controlling idea. Revise if necessary.

Some people go right on to college after high school; others take a year or more off to work or travel. Which do you think is the better choice? State your position and support it with specific reasons and examples.

_____

_____

_____

_____

Today's top professional athletes often have salaries and bonuses in the tens of millions of dollars. Do you think these athletes deserve such high compensation? Why or why not?
Explain your position and use specific reasons and examples.

_____

_____

_____

70

_____

_____

Write a *direct reference* topic sentence for each of the following writing prompts. Highlight your topic and controlling idea. Revise if necessary.

> Some educators argue that every child in every school should have access to computers. Others believe that the value of computers in the classroom is overrated and that computers may actually interfere with the learning process. In your opinion, how important are computers in the classroom? Use specific reasons and examples to explain your answer.

_____

_____

_____

_____

_____

> Many people believe that honesty is the best policy. In your opinion, is it ever okay to lie? Explain your answer using specific reasons and examples

_____

_____

_____

_____

_____

71

THINK 360°

PRACTICE: On a separate sheet of paper, brainstorm (using mapping, listing or free writing). Afterwards, below each of the writing prompts, create an *indirect reference* topic sentence. Highlight your topic and controlling idea. Revise if necessary.

> Some people are concerned that many teachers are not sufficiently qualified for the classroom and argue that they should be required to pass competency tests before they are allowed to teach. Do you agree? Why or why not? Explain your answer with specific reasons and examples.

_____

_____

_____

_____

_____

> Do you think the SAT or ACT exam is an accurate measure of a student's aptitude for college? Support your position with specific examples.

_____

_____

_____

_____

_____

_____

PRACTICE

Write an *indirect reference* topic sentence for each of the following writing prompts. Highlight your topic and controlling idea. Revise if necessary.

> Students who don't want to do their homework can find dozens of sites on the Internet that offer essays for sale. Do you think this is a legitimate business, or should these enterprises be shut down? Use specific reasons and examples to support your answer.

_____

_____

_____

_____

_____

> Should a parent be a child's disciplinarian, or a child's best friend? Take a position and explain your answer using specific reasons and examples.

_____

_____

_____

_____

_____

Ruby Tree Publishing ©

CHAPTER 6

TYPES OF EXAMPLES

In paragraph and essay development, examples support and explain the topic sentences and thesis statement. They are the "meat" of the essay and must be "carefully crafted" and "placed properly" in the paragraph structure to communicate effectively.

No one eats a sandwich with just bread and nothing in between. In many cases, people order sandwiches with a variety of deli meats, cheeses, vegetables, and condiments. The variety of flavors placed between the bread, meet the various nutritional needs and give variety to the palate. A person who consumes a sandwich that has a combination of bread, meat, cheese, lettuce tomatoes, mayonnaise, or mustard excites their taste buds in different ways. Sandwich making usually follows this process: the mayonnaise or mustard should be placed on the bread first, the meat should be included next, the cheese should be included afterwards and the vegetables are placed last.

The way that a sandwich is "carefully crafted" and items are "placed properly" for a flavorful sandwich, is quite similar to the way examples should be placed in a paragraph. After all, no one wants a sandwich with just mustard, and your essay grader doesn't want an essay with just your opinions.

There are different types of examples that should be used to create flavorful paragraphs and essays. These ideas are communicated via *facts, statistics, anecdotes and opinions*. Generally speaking, students favor answering writing prompts with their opinions, which are biased perspectives that are often rooted in learned ideas based upon their family values and life experiences. Their opinions, which are usually formed over time, are typically narrow-minded and untested. Therefore, the ideas are not able to be taken seriously because they lack true reasoning from a factual perspective. Opinions, at the college level, should be based upon factual information as the student moves from persuasive essays to argument essays.

Therefore, it is appropriate for test takers to use other mechanisms for developing their paragraphs. These ideas are found in the areas of FACTS, STATISTICS, and ANECDOTES. Through these types of examples, writers are able to test and extend their ideas by thinking of the opposing point of view. They are able to appeal to authority, or those who are credible figures via facts, statistics and anecdotes and discuss consequences for actions through factual historical data and anecdotes. Using examples in this way demonstrates critical thinking and helps form strong logical essays.

Examples are used to support the topic sentences.

The four primary types of examples are facts, opinions, statistics, and anecdotes. For exams, these types of details are appropriate and easy to use if presented properly. At least three examples, or supporting details, will provide you with appropriate development. A fair representation of each type of example will give you an edge on your standardized test essay.

Methods to for Body Paragraph Development

Anecdotes
Use a short story to prove a point and illustrate an idea by using vivid language and good plot structure to keep the reader engaged. In short, tell a REALLY good story that is fun to read and proves your point well.

Ruby Tree Publishing ©

Chronological order: time order, as things happen

Description: Descriptive details include adjectives and sensory detail based upon the five senses. Paired with anecdotes, it provides vivid details which help to keep your reader engaged in your work and literally able to "see" your point of view.

Order of location: in reference to where things are located

Anecdotes are a great resource when you are trying to explain a concept, but you don't have a lot of concrete facts to accompany them. Anecdotes are powerful, when they are paired with facts and statistics. They are more powerful when they are the stories of prominent people or people who are well respected. It is a good idea to research people who have a story you find inspirational. Their life story and ideas should reflect your value system, so when you are faced with a challenging writing prompt, you can call upon their experience and famous quotes to help you write more information about your topic.

Logical Patterns for Facts, Opinions and Statistics

Order of importance: go from most to least important or from least important to most important

Cause and Effect: Start with cause of a problem; continue with possible effects

Comparison: Explain a subject by showing how it is like another subject

Contrast: Explain a subject by showing how it is different from another subject

Paragraph Outline Structure

Topic Sentence – (main idea of the paragraph)

1st Example – (Supports the topic sentence)

2nd Example – (Supports the topic sentence)

3rd Example – (Supports the topic sentence)

Conclusion Statement – (Cincher/ Closing Statement)

ORGANIZATION AND STRUCTURE EXAMPLES WITHIN PARAGRAPHS

Writing essays is by no means formulaic. In other words, there is no formula that will guarantee you success on EVERY essay. However, there is a certain method that will work if you master it and expound upon it.

One of the major tenets of powerful essays is developing and organizing your examples under your topic sentence. Logical development in the brainstorming phase, which is when ideas are created and organized, can save time in revision, which happens after the first draft, or rough draft is written. Below is a formula that can serve as the basis for organizing and developing a paragraph in a logical, coherent way.

Deductive Reasoning

Deductive reasoning, in paragraph and essay writing, moves from general to the specific ideas. Therefore, topic sentences or thesis statements will be the lead idea in the paragraph because it is the broadest statement in paragraph. All other statements (examples) will connect to the main idea, and flow downward.

Ruby Tree Publishing ©

Deductive Reasoning

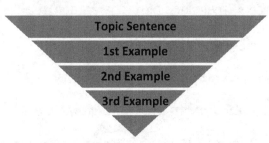

Topic Sentence

1st Example

2nd Example

3rd Example

In this pattern, the best or strongest example should be the first example, the second best should follow, and the weakest example should be the final detail. This model works well for those who are very structured in their thinking and very rarely stray from subject. It allows them the structure they need to move from general to specific in a very methodical type of way. Practical, logical, or deductive thinkers typically enjoy this model.

Inductive reasoning

In contrast to deductive reasoning, inductive reasoning moves from specific to general ideas in a paragraph. The writer arrives at a theory, perspective or topic sentence after explaining their examples first. In inductive reasoning, the writer offers an introductory statement, which serves as a backdrop or, general context, for what they will say throughout the paragraph. This method arrives at the topic sentence after reasoning through ideas as opposed to starting with the topic sentence initially. More intuitive, or people who reason through their feelings, would benefit from using this method because they do not have to address their topic sentence as they "feel their way" through the subject matter. When the inductive thinker writes, often the reader goes on a journey with the writer as they craft their work.

Ruby Tree Publishing ©

Inductive Reasoning

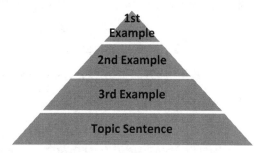

1st Example

2nd Example

3rd Example

Topic Sentence

Tips for Organization
EXAMPLES WITHIN PARAGRAPHS

Characteristics of Example 1

- The lead example (Example 1) should be strong.

    o It engages the reader early on so they are more likely to remain focused.

- It should have a transition word to indicate that it is the initial detail about the topic sentence.

    o It supports the topic sentence and provides more details. It should directly correlate to the topic sentence as it is the first supporting detail in the paragraph.

- It should have a transition word to indicate that it is the initial detail about the topic sentence.

- Sample transition words for lead off examples are **first, first of all, initially, to begin, in the first place, the first thing to remember, and for one thing.**

The example should be strong because it is the lead example. The example should be a fact, opinion, statistic, or anecdote. Ideally, it should link into the "introductory statement" as well.

Characteristics of Example 2

- It can be a new example or it can give further information about the first example.

- It should have a transition word to indicate it is the next detail or second detail in the paragraph. Sample transition words for interior examples are **secondly, additionally, also, in addition, similarly, like, and likewise.**

- To further explain the initial example, words such as **furthermore, accordingly, moreover, as a matter of fact, and by the same token**, can be used.

- It should be a fact, opinion, statistic, anecdote

Typically, anecdotes are smart to use as the second example because it is a short story used to prove a point. The short story can illustrate the first example and thereby provide further explanation about the topic sentence without falling into the trap of repetition. Instead the writer will give the reader illumination.

Characteristics of Example 3

It can be a new example or it can give further information about the first and/or second example.

- It should have a transition word to indicate it is the final detail or third detail in the paragraph. Sample transition words for closing examples are **thirdly, finally, in either case, for the most part, all things considered, and by and large.**

- As is the case in the second example, words such as *furthermore, accordingly, moreover, as a matter of fact, and by the same token,* can be used.

- It should be a fact, opinion, statistic, anecdote

Typically, a fact, opinion or statistic should be used here because it is meant to clarify your former examples or to solidify your support for the topic sentence. Therefore, it does not need to be long, but it needs to be clear and effective. Try to make it move your reader emotionally so that they remain engaged in your topic and have a clear understanding regarding your point of view.

Points to Remember
Paragraphs

There are three parts of a paragraph. Create the Topic Sentence by using the Writing Prompt

Introductory Statements: Contextualizes the paragraph and gets the attention of your reader.

Topic sentence: Use this formula for building a good topic sentence: a specific topic + a specific feeling or attitude.

Body of paragraph: Contains sentences that develop or explain the idea given in the topic sentence. Generally 5-7 sentences are necessary per paragraph.

Closing/Clincher sentence: Reminds the reader what the main idea of the paragraph is and what it means (why it is important). Closing sentences can also be a transition to the next paragraph.

Ruby Tree Publishing ©

THINK 360°

PRACTICE: On a separate sheet of paper, brainstorm (using mapping, listing or free writing). Afterwards, on the lines following each of the writing prompts, create a *direct* or an *indirect reference* topic sentence. Highlight your topic and controlling idea. Finally, create examples to support your topic sentence. Review the paragraph development checklist. Revise if necessary.

Practice Prompts
Paragraph Development

Prepare to write an effective paragraph based upon the following writing prompt. Please use the Paragraph Development Checklist to check your work.

The Internet

Write an essay illustrating how the Internet has been either beneficial or harmful in a specific area. For instance (these examples are not required topics), write about how the Internet has made research much easier for students, OR write about how the Internet has given predators easy access to minors.

_____

_____

_____

_____

_____

_____

_____

_____

_____

_____

Paragraph Development
Checklist

___Brainstorm

___ Outline

___ Do you have an introductory phrase/ what kind_____

___ Does your topic sentence discuss the topic

___ Does your topic sentence have a controlling idea

___ How many facts

___ How many statistics

___ How many anecdotes

___ How many opinions

___ Do you consider an opposing opinion in your argument (Y/N)

___ Do you use transition words between your ideas

___ How many sentences do you have _____

___ What is your pattern of organization_____

___ Did you use inductive or deductive reasoning (circle)

___ Do you have a conclusion statement_____

___ Do you have unity in your ideas (Y/N)

___ Are you focused on the subject of the prompt (Y/N)

Practice Prompts
Paragraph Development
Prompt 2

Prepare to write an effective paragraph based upon the following writing prompt. Please use the Paragraph Development Checklist to check your work.

Leadership
Who makes a better leader: someone who is loved, or someone who is feared? Take a position and explain your answer.

_____

_____

_____

_____

_____

_____

_____

_____

_____

_____

_____

_____

_____

_____

_____

_____

_____

_____

_____

_____

Paragraph Development
Checklist

___Brainstorm

___ Outline

___ Do you have an introductory phrase/ what kind_____

___ Does your topic sentence discuss the topic

___ Does your topic sentence have a controlling idea

___ How many facts

___ How many statistics

___ How many anecdotes

___ How many opinions

___ Do you consider an opposing opinion in your argument (Y/N)

___ Do you use transition words between your ideas

___ How many sentences do you have _____

___ What is your pattern of organization_____

___ Did you use inductive or deductive reasoning (circle)

___ Do you have a conclusion statement_____

___ Do you have unity in your ideas (Y/N)

___ Are you focused on the subject of the prompt (Y/N)

Practice Prompts
Paragraph Development
Prompt 3

Prepare to write an effective paragraph based upon the following writing prompt. Please use the Paragraph Development Checklist to check your work.

Education

Is a good education a right or a privilege? Why do you think so? Use specific reasons and examples to explain your answer.

Paragraph Development Checklist

____Brainstorm

____ Outline

____ Do you have an introductory phrase/ what kind_____

____ Does your topic sentence discuss the topic

____ Does your topic sentence have a controlling idea

____ How many facts

____ How many statistics

____ How many anecdotes

____ How many opinions

____ Do you consider an opposing opinion in your argument (Y/N)

____ Do you use transition words between your ideas

____ How many sentences do you have _____

____ What is your pattern of organization_____

____ Did you use inductive or deductive reasoning (circle)

____ Do you have a conclusion statement_____

____ Do you have unity in your ideas (Y/N)

____ Are you focused on the subject of the prompt (Y/N)

CHAPTER 7

INTRODUCTORY STATEMENTS
and
CONCLUSION STATEMENTS

Introductory statements have forever been relegated to the typical "attention grabber" or "shocking statement". As students prepare for higher education, they will have to evolve into true scholars who use a variety of scholarly introductory statements to truly get their professor's attention. Conclusion statements, conversely, leave a lasting impression in the reader's mind. It is not widely taught, nor is it really "expected" in essay writing. However, a well crafted conclusion statement signals to the reader that a paragraph is ending, and it gives the reader something to ponder. It is a valuable tool for elite writers.

Introductory Statements

These introductory statements are no longer the "tabloid" type of headline that speaks to a large audience. Instead, the "lead in" should have a variety of faces to appeal to a variety of graders. The type of introductory statement should be chosen based upon the audience who will render a grade. It is the test taker's responsibility to grab the attention of the scholar who is reading their essay.

Types of Introductory Statements

Use an anecdote which is a short story used to prove a point. The story should grab the reader's attention, be short, mysterious, sad, humorous, or funny.

Use statistics which may be shocking or meant to solicit an emotional response from your reader.

Use a quotation from a famous and/or respectable person. A quote from your parent or family member may not elicit as much as a response as a quote from President Kennedy, but it will at least give the reader an opportunity to see people who have influenced your life's perspective. Try to memorize 10 quotes.

Use a rhetorical question. Make sure that the point of the question is requires the reader to reflect in a way that favors your thesis statement.

Use historical/factual data. This will give you a deep introduction chalked full of data which will make you credible and will score high points with the reader. Remember, it must be facts or historical information that can be proven. Your audience is well educated.

Use wit or trivia to serve as an eye-catcher. Because your audience is well educated, they will appreciate your intellect and ability to "think outside of the box."

Prepare to write introductory statements

It is important for students do preliminary reading to learn facts. It is also good to learn a list of quotes that can be used as use as "go to" introductory statements. To make your research count, figure out what is important to you in life and have 5-10 quotes from famous, credible, noteworthy people who feel the same way. The quotes don't have to be long – just good. To research quotes, simply use a search engine and keying in the name of a "family value" that is important to you and the word "quote".

Ruby Tree Publishing ©

A simple search can give you a lot to use in your introductory statements. The next section shows the results of a search using the keywords "hard work" and "quote"...

Sample Search Engine Results

Hard Work Quotes : Finest Quotes
Hard Work Quotes. Inspirational **quotes** about **Hard Work.** Let these words of greatminds inspire you and help you to achieve your goals and live a fulfilling life.
www.**finestquotes.com**/select_**quote**-category-**Hard**%20Work... - Cached

• **Hard Work Quote - Quotes Quotations**
Hard Work Quote: a collection. Part of a special section on inspirational and motivational **quotes**. Also find lists, databases, and resources for **quotes** and **quotations**.
quotations.about.com/cs/inspirationquotes/a/Effort2.htm - Cached

• **Hard Work Quotes - BrainyQuote**
Hard Work Quotes from BrainyQuote, an extensive collection of **quotations** by famous authors, celebrities, and newsmakers.
www.**brainyquote.com**/quotes/keywords/**hard_work**.html   -   Cached
More results from brainyquote.com »

• **Hard Work quotes**
Hard Work quotes, **Hard Work**, topic, topics, ... It's a test of ultimate will The heartbreak climb uphill Got to pick up the pace If you want to stay in the race More ...
thinkexist.com/quotations/**hard_work** - Cached

• **Quotes About Hard Work**
Quotes About **Hard Work**: a collection. Part of a special section on inspirational and motivational **quotes**. Also find lists, databases, and resources for **quotes** and ...
quotations.about.com/cs/inspirationquotes/a/Effort6.htm - Cached

• **Hard Work Quotes - Woopidoo Business Success - Motivational ...**
Hard Work quotes about **working hard** from business experts, financial authorities, and motivational authors.
www.**woopidoo.com**/business_quotes/**hard-work**.htm - Cached

93

- **Hard Work Quotes | Hard Work Pays off Quotes and Sayings**
Inspiring **quotes** about **Hard Working**. **Hard Work** does pay off and these **Hard work quotes** will inspire you to continue **working hard** without thinking about the result
www.**allfamousquotes.net/hard-work**-quotes - Cached

- **Hard Work Quotes & Sayings :: Finest Quotes**
Famous **quotes** with keyword **Hard Work**. Let these words of greatminds inspire you and help you to achieve your goals and live a fulfilling life.
www.**finestquotes.com/quote_**with-keyword-**Hard**%20Work-page... - Cached

- **Effort Quotes, Motivational Sayings about Hard Work, Work Ethic**
Quotations about effort and **hard work**, from The **Quote** Garden.
www.**quotegarden.com**/effort.html - Cached

- **Hard Work Quotes | Quotes about Hard Work | Sayings about ...**
Browse **Hard Work quotes** and famous **quotes** about **Hard Work** on SearchQuotes.com.
www.**searchquotes.com**/quotes/about/**Hard_Work** - Cached

Sample List of Quotes

The following quotes came from the first website on the list, *FinestQuotes.com.*

I do not know anyone who has gotten to the top without hard work. That is the recipe. It will not always get you to the top, but it will get you pretty near.

Margaret Thatcher

I'm a great believer in luck and I find the harder I work, the more I have of it.

Thomas Jefferson

You'll never succeed in idealizing hard work. Before you can dig mother earth you've got to take off your ideal

94

jacket. The harder a man works, at brute labor, the thinner becomes his idealism, the darker his mind.

D. H. Lawrence

If the power to do hard work is not a skill, it's the best possible substitute for it.

James A. Garfield

If hard work were such a wonderful thing, surely the rich would have kept it all to themselves.

Lane Kirkland

When you live for a strong purpose, then hard work isn't an option. It's a necessity.

Steve Pavlina

There is no substitute for hard work.

Thomas Alva Edison

Unless you are willing to drench yourself in your work beyond the capacity of the average man, you are just not cut out for positions at the top.

J.C. Penney

To find more quotes, visit FinestQuotes.com.

Conclusion Statements

The conclusion statement is similar to a conclusion paragraph in that it summarizes the paragraph or, if it is serving as a body paragraph, it can lead the reader into another body paragraph.

It summarizes the topic sentence while it provides closure for the paragraph. In essays, it transitions the reader from one paragraph to the next paragraph.

In many cases, it should have a conclusion transition word. Sample conclusion words are: ***overall, all in all, in the end, in short, in a word, all things considered, in the final analysis, in essence, and altogether.*** A word of caution, many instructors do not like conclusion transition words. Make sure you find your instructor's preference before writing.

There is no mystery to writing a conclusion statement. Use them to guide your reader to the end of your paragraph.

Introductory statements and Conclusion statements open and close your paragraphs. The introduction is important because it gets the reader's attention and hooks them into your mode of thinking. The conclusion statement allows the reader to know that they have come to the end of your idea and that they should remember all that was written. Both the beginning and end of your paragraph leaves an impression on the reader. The idea is also the case for the introduction and conclusion paragraphs.

CHAPTER 8

INTRODUCTONS AND CONCLUSIONS

Writing prompts typically beg for an introduction in standardized tests and course based written tests. It is important to allow the reader to connect with your work so that they can remain engaged in your ideas. A well crafted introduction makes a good impression. As the old saying goes, "You only get one time to make a good first impression." Making a good first impression can "make" or "break" your essay. Therefore, the introductory statement needs to be well thought out in the introduction paragraph of an essay. Unlike the single paragraph assignment, the reader will have to engage your work for a longer period of time. It is essential that you formulate your introduction to keep them engaged as you lead them into your thesis statement.

Thesis Statements in Introductions

The **thesis statement** is the main idea of the introduction paragraph because it is the main idea of the essay. It is a broad statement that serves as the guiding statement; it also serves as the main idea of your essay. Like the topic sentence of a standard paragraph, it has a **topic** which comes from the writing prompt. It has a **controlling idea** which is the author's attitude or perspective about the topic.

There are two ways to approach the introduction paragraph of an essay. The difference involves the placement of the main idea. In this case, the main idea is the thesis statement and it may be placed at the beginning or end of the paragraph.

Topic Sentences in Introductions

Topic sentences expound upon your thesis in the introduction paragraph. While some students don't include them at all in their introductions, other students allow them to set their paper into a logical format. The topic sentences, then, serve as "major points" in the introductory paragraph. They give reasons, ideas of explanations that validate the thesis statement.

The Role of Parents

Should a parent be a child's disciplinarian, or a child's best friend? Take a position and explain your answer using specific reasons and examples.

Parental Appeal

"Discipline is a symbol of caring to a child. He needs guidance. If there is love, there is no such thing as being too tough with a child. A parent must also not be afraid to hang himself. If you have never been hated by your child, you have never been a parent." Bette Davis, a starlet of the 1930's and award winning actress in the 1970's and 80's, with this quote, promotes an idea that is true to the heart of many. Parents are required to help their children grow into the responsible adults they need to be. Parents do not give in to peer pressure, nor do they indulge their children's wish to be "cool". This is the function of a friend in a child's life because being accepted and being invited to remain in good standing is an act of friendship. Instead of focusing on popularity, parents should focus on the long term results of the decisions their children make. **Parents should rear their children through the emotions of love of respect and not through the need to be accepted as a friend.** By implementing tough love and mutual respect, the parent will achieve the love and honor that any parent, child or even friend would desire.

98

Sample Introduction Paragraph Analysis
Inductive Reasoning

The Thesis Statement "Parents should rear their children through the emotions of love and respect and through the need to be accepted as a friend" is strategically placed at end of the paragraph to create emphasis on the thesis statement. Let's look at the difference in emphasis when placed near the beginning of the introduction near the introductory statement.

Parental Appeal

"Discipline is a symbol of caring to a child. He needs guidance. If there is love, there is no such thing as being too tough with a child. A parent must also not be afraid to hang himself. If you have never been hated by your child, you have never been a parent." Bette Davis', a starlet of the 1930's and award winning actress in the 1970's and 80's, with this quote, promotes an idea that is true to the heart of many. **Parents should rear their children through the emotions of love of respect and not through the need to be accepted as a friend.** Parents are required to help their children grow into the responsible adults they need to be. Parents do not give in to peer pressure, nor do they indulge their children's wish to be "cool". This is the function of a friend in a child's life. Being accepted and being invited to remain in good standing is an act of friendship. Instead of focusing on popularity, parents should focus on the long term results of the decisions their children make. By implementing tough love and mutual respect, the parent will achieve the love and honor that any parent, child or even friend would desire.

Sample Introduction Paragraph Analysis
Deductive Reasoning

In the second sample paragraph, the subtle yet noticeable placement of the thesis delivers the same information in a new way. The point of the essay is given early, and it leaves little to the imagination. Instead, the writer is predicable and the reader expects exactly what is given. There are three points that follow the thesis and the conclusion statement reminds the reader of the main idea of the essay because it reflects the guiding thought of the thesis.

Sample Introduction Outlines

Introductory Statement
A. "Discipline is a symbol of caring to a child. He needs guidance. If there is love, there is no such thing as being too tough with a child. A parent must also not be afraid to hang himself. If you have never been hated by your child, you have never been a parent." Bette Davis', a starlet of the 1930's and award winning actress in the 1970's and 80's, with this quote, promotes and idea that is true to the heart of many.

Topic Sentence 1 (Point 1)
B. Parents are required to help their children grow into the responsible adults they need to be.

Topic Sentence (Point 2)
C. Parents do not give in to peer pressure, nor do they indulge their children's wish to be "cool".

Topic Sentence (Point 3)
D. Instead of focusing on popularity, parents should focus on the long term results of the decisions their children make.

Thesis Statement
E. Parents should rear their children through the emotions of love of respect as a parent and not through a need to be accepted as a friend.
Conclusion Statement
E. By implementing tough love and mutual respect, the parent will achieve the love and honor that any parent, child or even friend would desire.

Introductory Statement

A. "Discipline is a symbol of caring to a child. He needs guidance. If there is love, there is no such thing as being too tough with a child. A parent must also not be afraid to hang himself. If you have never been hated by your child, you have never been a parent." Bette Davis', a starlet of the 1930's and award winning actress in the 1970's and 80's, with this quote, promotes and idea that is true to the heart of many.

Thesis Statement

E. Parents should rear their children through the emotions of love of respect as a parent and not through a need to be accepted as a friend.

Topic Sentence 1 (Point 1)

B. Parents are required to help their children grow into the responsible adults they need to be.

Topic Sentence (Point 2)

C. Parents do not give in to peer pressure, nor do they indulge their children's wish to be "cool".

Topic Sentence (Point 3)

D. Instead of focusing on popularity, parents should focus on the long term results of the decisions their children make.

Conclusion Statement

E. By implementing tough love and mutual respect, the parent will achieve the love and honor that any parent, child or even friend would desire.

Ruby Tree Publishing ©

Introduction Paragraph Structures

Inductive Reasoning — **Late Thesis Statement Announcement**

A. *Introductory Statement*
B. Topic Sentence 1
C. Topic Sentence 2
D. Topic Sentence 3
E. Thesis Statement
F. Conclusion Statement

Deductive Reasoning — **Early Thesis Statement Announcement**

A. *Introductory Statement*
B. Thesis Statement
C. Topic Sentence 1
D. Topic Sentence 2
E. Topic Sentence 3
F. Conclusion Statement

Conclusion Paragraphs

Conclusion paragraphs to some are an enigma, and to others they are not mysterious at all. Instead they are a mundane and unnecessary practice when composing essays. The point of the conclusion paragraph is close out your essay and to recall your general points of your essay. For test questions, it should solidify your position on the writing prompt. It should include a final thought about your subject and it should make a lasting impression on your reader.

Reflect and Project

The conclusion paragraph should reflect – summarize the major points of the essay (including the thesis) and it should project – call to action and excite the reader to do something in the future. Some suggest asking a question in the final paragraph to leave the reader with an issue that they will need to resolve. This is another way of projecting the point of your paper into future conversations. Finally, a clever way of concluding your essay is to refer back to the *introductory statement* in your introduction paragraph. This idea promotes essay unity and it also gives the writer a second opportunity to reinforce the point of the introductory statement. If the statement is ironic or humorous then a witty response to it in the conclusion is idea. If you create a lasting impression on the reader, then you have accomplished your goal. All of these methods are appropriate for creating well crafted and meaningful conclusions.

Conclusion Paragraph Structure
A. Thesis Statement (Reflect and Project)
B. Topic Sentence 1 (Reflect and Project)
C. Topic Sentence 2 (Reflect and Project)
D. Topic Sentence 3 (Reflect and Project)
E. Conclusion Statement (Reflect and Project)

THINK 360°

Practice Writing Introductions and Conclusions

Below are 5 writing prompts. Write an introduction for each of the writing prompts. Remember, you can use a variety of introductory statements and either inductive (late thesis) or deductive (early thesis) to create your paragraph. Remember to state your major points, if you think that you will get off track and stray from subject.

(If you need help with thesis statements, See Chapter 5)

After you have written the introduction, create a conclusion using the "reflect and project" model. Remember the introduction and conclusion paragraph are like book ends, so your information should correlate. Later, you can add in body or topic paragraphs to complete your masterpiece.

Practice Writing Prompts
Writing Introductions and Conclusions

1. Is there something that you believe is truly worth fighting for? Write an essay persuading others that this cause is worth a fight.

2. Good habits improve our physical, emotional, and/or financial health. Select one of your good habits and write an essay persuading readers to make that habit a part of their lives.

3. Discuss the importance of pride in one's work.

4. Explain the meaning of diversity.

5. Discuss a public health concern that you believe is serious enough to warrant immediate attention.

CHAPTER 9

EFFECTIVE EDITING

There are several things students need to know to edit effectively. However, for standardized test and other types of tests or written assignments, the grader is looking primarily for content, but does not want to be distracted by grammar and editing errors. Therefore, it is important that students review their written work to proofread for spelling, capitalization, grammar, usage and punctuation. In this chapter, you will learn the primary mechanics of editing. There is a vast amount of information regarding grammar that this book does not address as it goes beyond the scope of its general intent which is to teach you how to be successful at answering and delivering appropriate responses to writing prompts.

Nevertheless, you must know how to polish your essay so that it finished and well stated. The fourth step in the writing process is editing, which is where the author proofreads their work for minor, yet important mistakes. To edit sentences correctly, you must know sentence structure.

To write an effective essay or paragraph, you should use sentence variety consisting of simple sentences, compound sentences, complex sentences, and compound complex sentences. The main thing to remember is that the sentence must be complete.

Complete sentences require at least one complete thought. The complete thoughts are communicated through what is known as an independent clause, or a **simple sentence**. Other types of sentences are **compound sentences** which include at least 2 or more independent clauses, **complex sentences** which include a dependent clause and an independent clause, and a **compound complex sentence** which includes a dependent clause, and at least 2 independent clauses.

Simple Sentences have a **subject**, which is the "who or what" that is performing the action, or it may have the "who or what" that is being described. The subject of the sentence is usually a noun, pronoun, gerund or infinitive. Each sentence must also have a predicate which includes the **verb** or action in the sentence.

A **noun** is a person, place, thing or idea. It includes words like *mother, El Paso, book, or time.*

They have a few categories such as **common nouns** which are nonspecific nouns which can refer any general person, place thing or idea. A few common nouns are *boy, girl, dog, socks and the internet.*

There are also, **proper nouns** which reference a specific person, place thing or idea. These words require a capital letter. Examples are *John, Dallas, Range Rover, and Google.*

Pronouns are also common subjects as they replace nouns with words such as: *he, she, it, they, I, we, us, him, her, me, our, and theirs.*

Gerunds are verbs that have an "ing" ending but are used as nouns. For instance, "Painting relaxes me". In this sentence, the idea of painting relaxes me. Therefore, painting is the subject of the sentence although it is an action. It is the idea of the action that is the subject of the sentence. Therefore, it is a gerund as opposed to a regular noun.

Infinitives are also a subject that is formed from a verb. Infinitive phrases include "to + the verb" as is the case in "to work", "to dance", and "to sing".

Verbs are not only found in the subject of the sentence. In fact, verbs, in the predicate of the sentence, serve as the engine that moves the subject in clear direction. Either the subject is moved by action or it is described by using a **linking verb**.

Ruby Tree Publishing ©

Common **action verbs** are, *jump, walk run and sing.* These words clearly show the subject engaging in some sort of activity. For example, Mark and John *walk* to school together on Tuesdays. When you visualize this statement, you can clearly see to boys engaged in the activity of walking.

However, there are other verbs which help the subject have meaning through the vehicle of description. These words are commonly "be" verbs which speak to a state of being. Common **"be" verbs** include, *are, is, was, were, being, becoming, became.* Other common linking verbs are rooted in sensory material. **Sensory material** deals with the five senses. They include words such as feel, taste, sound, look, appear, seem, smell etc. Linking verbs, or descriptive words, link the subject to the words that describe them.

Consider the example, "Houston is the fourth largest city in the United States". In this case, Houston is being described as the fourth largest city in the United States. Look at this statement. "Pappadeaux's vanilla cheesecake tastes like a traditional New York Style Cheesecake; however, it feels light and creamy and is not heavy or bulky. In this sentence, you can see that the vanilla cheesecake is being compared to a New York Style Cheesecake through the sense of "taste". In the second part of the sentence, you can see that it is being described as light and fluffy. Linking verbs are key words to help you establish sentences that require description.

It is important to know sentence structure as it is helpful to determine the various types of sentences. Sentence variety in an essay makes the information more palatable. Going back to the sandwich example from Chapter 5, no one wants to have just mustard on their sandwich, and graders don't want to read a paper chalked with simple sentences. Variety is the spice of life! Therefore, sentences should have variety and they should be well written.

Ruby Tree Publishing ©

TYPES OF SENTENCES

Find the following words or phrases in the chapter. Record their definitions and any useful information in the following section.

Simple sentences, also known as independent clauses, have a subject and a predicate.

Compound sentences include 2 independent clauses, or simple sentences, and are joined by a coordinating conjunction.

Coordinating Conjunctions are words that join words, phrases or clauses.

For, **A**nd, **N**or, **B**ut, **O**r, **Y**et, **S**o

These words are commonly known as the *FANBOYS*. They create longer sentences when they combine simple sentences, or independent clauses, together.

Here is an example.

Austin has worked hard to establish a stable economy for its city, *but* Dallas has managed to create more jobs during the recession.

Complex Sentences include an independent and dependent clause.

Subordinating conjunctions, when attached to a clause, creates a dependent clause. Common words subordinating conjunctions are:

After, Although, As, Because, Before, Even if, Even though, In order that, Once, Provided that, Rather than, Since, So that, Than, That, Though, Unless, Until, When, Whenever, Where, Whereas, Whatever, While and Why.

The subordinating conjunctions serve as transition between ideas in the dependent and independent clauses. It creates a relationship which shows, time, place or a cause and effect relationship.

Ruby Tree Publishing ©

Consider the following sentence.

Even though Houston is considered the energy capital of Texas, it is nick named the "Bayou City".

The dependent clause in the sentence has the subordinating conjunction even though. The complete dependent clause is "Even though Houston is considered the energy capital of Texas." The independent clause in the sentence comes after the comma. The independent clause reads "it is nick named the "Bayou City" The entire sentence is a compound sentence.

SUBJECT VERB AGREEMENT

Subjects and verbs must agree in number and tense. For **singular subjects** (which are subjects that include only one person, place, thing or idea - *he, she, and it*) **agree with verbs that end in "s"**

Here is an example.

The <u>child</u> **cries** excessively when her mother leaves the room.

Notice that the subject "child" refers to one child and the verb "cries" ends in "s".

When the subject is plural (more than one) then the verb should not have the "s" or "es" suffix.

For **plural subjects** which are subjects that include more than one person, place, thing or idea – *we, they and you* (both singular and plural you), the verb *does not* include an "s" or "es"

Here is an example.

The <u>children</u> **cry** excessively when their mother leaves the room.
Notice that the subject "child" refers to more than one child and the verb "cry" does not have a suffix.

113

COMMAS

There are important rules to remember when editing your paragraphs and essays. There are more comma rules, but the three listed below are the "must know" basic comma rules.

1. Use commas to separate items in a list of three or more.

Example: I like apples, oranges, and bananas.

2. Use a comma to separate independent clauses (simple sentences) when joining them to form a compound sentence. The comma goes before the coordinating conjunction.

Example: The University of Texas and Texas A&M are well known rivals, but Texas Southern University and Prairie View A&M have a long standing rivalry as well.

3. Use a comma to separate dependent from independent clauses in complex sentences. When the dependent clause comes first in a complex sentence, place a comma after the last word in the dependent clause.

Example: If you eat breakfast in the morning, you will have more energy.

4. Use commas to introduce prepositional phrases and transitions

Example: At the end of a long day, I need to relax.

Example: For example, John jogs every evening after work.

5. Use commas to insert words or phrases that are not necessary to the sentence. Put a comma on both sides of the word or phrase.

Example: Mary and Sam, unfortunately, will not be able to join us this evening.

Example: Beans, like other forms of fiber, are good for your digestive system.

Remember!

After you have completely revised and edited your essay or paragraph, the final step of the writing process is present a final draft. It is clear of errors and structured appropriately. If possible, avoid writing a new draft of your essay unless your instructor requests it. Instead simply double space your first draft to make revision and editing easier. Make your changes in the blank lines between your text. Revision and editing polish your work; it makes it easy for the reader to understand your logic and language patterns. These important proofreading activities are the key to your essay's success.

For more on information grammar, visit the *Guide to Grammar* website sponsored by the Capital Community College Foundation. This website is quite helpful if you want to learn additional rules to improve your grammar or complete practice questions to test your skills.

www.grammar.commnet.edu/grammar/

PRACTICE PROMPT EXERCISES

PRACTICE: Editing and Revision are key parts of essay writing. Can you edit and revise this student's essay for mistakes in content and sentence formation? Please re-write the essay correctly on a separate sheet of paper.

Writing Prompt
"Love"
In an essay, explain how to develop a romantic love relationship based upon the three stages of love known as agape "an unconditional love", philio "a brotherly love" and eros, "romantic love".

Three Chapters of Love

There are three stages of love in developing an intimate relationship. The first stage in developing an intimate relationship would be establishing Agape love. The second stage of development in an intimate relationship is "brotherly love" which is also known as Philio love. The third stage of a fully developed relationship would be "passionate love" commonly known as Eros. In the end, if you follow these steps you will have a strong and intimate relationship.

The first stage in developing an intimate relationship would be establishing Agape love. Having the respect for one another, listening to what each other has to say about themselves. Getting the chance to know each other and having deep feelings. Agape love is family love we have unconditional love for one another. Having emotion and feeling such as love for animals. For example, if someone ran over a cat and killed it in the middle of the road you would have some kind of sympathy for the cat. Well that's what you call Agape love. In all Agape love is unconditional love, and would help you in an intimate relationship.

The second stage of development in an intimate relationship is "brotherly love" which is also known as Philio love. You become great friends with one another and, open up to each other. This is when you really get to know each other. You share pass experience with one another. You begin to express your strong feelings, and inner thoughts. At this stage, we begin to feel comfortable with one another and become very expressive with one another.

117

The third stage of a fully developed relationship would be "passionate love" commonly known as Eros. Within this stage, you begin to have sexual desire one another such as, sharing romantic evenings together. Often at times begin to have butterflies in your stomach feeling the emotion. Getting aroused with each other and sharing intimate sex. At this stage, we come to realize how sacred the meaning of Eros turns out to be.

In conclusion using these steps will help to build a long term relationship. Agape love is the best first step in an intimate relationship because couples should have the secure and feel comfortable. It will help you bond and create that structure of a long term relationship. Philio love is the second best step for a relationship. You will become best friends, be able to trust one another and have great conversation. Eros is the third best step for an intimate relationship. You become passionate with your spouse. If couples build a great foundation based upon these three stages of love, they will succeed.

Ruby Tree Publishing ©

Quiz Yourself

1. What is the subject of this essay based upon the writing prompt?

2. What is the author's controlling idea?

3. What is the thesis of this essay?

4. What is the purpose of this essay? Is it to convince or to explain?

5. What are the topic sentences of each of the body paragraphs?

6. Does she properly develop each of the paragraphs? What types of examples does she use? How many of each?

Facts   _____

Opinions   _____

Statistics   _____

Anecdotes   _____

Writing Prompt
"Love"

In an essay, explain how to develop a romantic love relationship based upon the three stages of love known as agape "an unconditional love", philio "a brotherly love" and eros, "romantic love".

Brainstorm, write, revise and edit your work.
Don't forget to double space so you will have room to edit.

Ruby Tree Publishing ©

WRITE AN SHORT ESSAY OUTLINE FOR *BOTH* OF THE FOLLOWING WRITING PROMPTS:

Short Essay Prompt 1

Should single parents, who are physically and mentally able to work but have young children (9 yrs. old or less), be forced off welfare?

Short Essay Prompt 2

Should the United States who is a country of democracy and freedom continue to keep the same traditional husband and wife gender roles in the home, or is it time to allow moms to be the primary breadwinner while dads remain home with the children?

SHORT ANSWER PRACTICE

WRITE A SHORT PARAGRAPH ON THE NEXT PAGE WHERE YOU ANSWER THE FOLLOWING QUESTIONS.

IDENTIFY THE SUBJECT, AUDIENCE, AND PURPOSE FOR WRITING BASED UPON THE WRITING PROMPTS. WRITE A SEPARATE ANSWER FOR EACH PROMPT.

CHECK FOR UNITY FOCUS.

DO ALL OF YOUR IDEAS SPEAK TO THE THESIS STATEMENT?

DO YOU YOUR TOPIC SENTENCES DIRECTLY RELATE TO THE SUBJECT PROVIDED BY THE WRITING PROMPTS?

Ruby Tree Publishing ©

ESSAY STRUCTURE ASSIGNMENT (TOPIC 1)

Should single parents, who are physically and mentally able to work but have young children (9 yrs. old or less), be forced off welfare?

_____

_____

_____

_____

_____

_____

_____

_____

_____

_____

_____

_____

_____

_____

_____

_____

_____

_____

_____

_____

_____

_____

_____

_____

_____

_____

ESSAY STRUCTURE ASSIGNMENT (TOPIC 2)

Should the United States who is a country of democracy and freedom continue to keep the same traditional husband and wife gender roles in the home, or is it time to allow moms to be the primary breadwinner while dads remain home with the children?

_____

_____

_____

_____

_____

_____

_____

_____

_____

_____

_____

_____

_____

_____

_____

_____

_____

_____

_____

_____

_____

_____

Ruby Tree Publishing ©

Resources

Advantogy. Learning Styles Online. Web. 8 Jan. 2011.

Beilock, Sian L. and Gerardo Ramirez. "Writing About Test Worries Boost Exam Performance in the Classroom". *Sciencemag.org.* 14 Jan. 2011. Web. 24. Jan. 2011

Cooper, Sheila and Rosemary Patton. *Writing Logically, Thinking Critically, 5th ed.* New York: Pearson Longman, 2005. Print.

"Hard Work Quotes." *FinestQuotes.com*. Web. 24 Jan. 2011.

Hutton, Shannon. "Helping Kinesthetic Learners Succeed." Education.com. 20 Nov. 2007. Web. Jan. 12, 2011.

---. "Helping Auditory Learners Succeed." Education.com. Web. Jan. 12, 2011.

---. "Helping Visual Learners Succeed." Education.com Web. Jan. 12, 2011.

Learning Express. *501 Writing Prompts*. New York: Learning Express, LLC. 2003. Web.

Owen, Ross. Walter Pauk *How to Study in College, 8th ed.* New York: Houghton Mifflin, 2006. Print

"Sample Test Questions." *ACT/COMPASS*. 2011. Web. 16 Jan. 2011.

The Guide to Grammar and Writing. *The Capital Community College Foundation. 2011. Web. 20 Jan. 2011*